The Voyage of the "Dawn Treader"

A guide to C. S. Lewis' Novel
By
Shan Gillard

Cover Illustration by Shan Gillard

ISBN: 1484048784
ISBN-13: 978-1484048788

For Melodye, Elisa and Shona, Who loved the Chronicles of Narnia

CONTENTS

AUTHOR BIOGRAPHY

Clive Staples Lewis (known to his friends as "Jack") was born on November 29, 1898, in Belfast, Northern Ireland to Albert J. and Florence Lewis. His brother Warren (Warnie) was three years older than he. In 1905 the family moved to their new home, "Little Lea," on the outskirts of Belfast.

Flora Lewis died of cancer in 1908, and Jack entered Wynyard School in England, where his brother Warnie had been attending since 1905. Due to respiratory problems, he was enrolled in Campbell College, Belfast in 1910, and eventually sent to Cherbourg School, Malvern, England in 1911. Malvern was famous as a health resort, and Warnie was enrolled at Malvern College. While at boarding school, Jack was introduced to the occult by one of his teachers, and eventually became an atheist.

In 1914 Lewis met Arthur Greeves, who, next to his brother, became his closest friend. He also began to study under W.T. Kirkpatrick ("The Great Knock"), and in 1916 won a scholarship to Oxford College. He was a student at Oxford from April 26 until September of 1916.

Lewis enlisted in the British army and was billeted in Keble College, Oxford, for officer's training. His roommate was Edward Courtnay Francis "Paddy" Moore. Lewis was wounded during the Battle of Arras on April 15, 1918, was returned to duty in October, and discharged in December 1918. Paddy Moore was killed in battle. "Death in Battle," published in the February, 1919 issue of *Reveille*, was Lewis' first published work. From January 1919 until June 1924 he resumed his studies at Oxford.

In 1920, Paddy Moore's mother and sister moved to Oxford, and Lewis lived with them from June 1921 on. In 1930 they purchased "The Kilns." The title to the property belonged to Mrs. Moore, with both Jack and Warren Lewis having rights of life tenancy.

From October 1924 until May 1925, Lewis served as philosophy tutor at University College. In May he was elected a Fellow of Magdalen College, Oxford, where he served as a tutor in English language and Literature until 1954.

In 1931 Lewis became a Christian after having had a long talk with two of his friends, J.R.R. Tolkien and Hugo Dyson. The talk took place in the evening, and is recorded in *They Stand Together*. Lewis recorded the following day's events in *Surprised by Joy*: "When we (Warnie and Jack) set out (by motorcycle to the Whipsnade Zoo) I did not believe that Jesus Christ was the Son of God, and when we reached the zoo I did."

In 1933, Lewis began having regular meetings with a group of friends who were writers, calling themselves the Inklings. Included in this group were J.R.R. Tolkien, Lewis' brother Warren, Hugo Dyson, Charles Williams, Dr. Robert Havard, Owen Barfield, Weville Coghill and others.

Lewis became a prolific writer and a leading apologist (one who defends the Christian faith). He published *The Screwtape Letters* in 1941, *The Abolition of Man* in 1943, *Mere Christianity* and *The Great* Divorce in 1945. Out *of the Silent Planet*, the first novel in his Space Trilogy, was published in 1938; *Perelandra*, the second novel of the Trilogy, in 1943, and *That Hideous Strength* in 1945.

Of course, *The Chronicles of Narnia*, a series of seven books which continue to enjoy tremendous popularity, was published between 1950 and 1956. The concept for *The Chronicles of Narnia* was born when Lewis opened his home to some of the English children who were sent to live in the countryside in order to escape the bombing of the British cities. Some of the children became fascinated with a wardrobe in his home, believing it led to another world. Having read about such a magic wardrobe when he was a child in *The Aunt and Anabel* by Edith Nesbit, he was captivated by the idea.

In 1952 Lewis met Joy Davidman Gresham, who was fifteen years his junior, for the first time. She had converted to Christianity from Judaism in 1948 in part as a result of reading his books. They were married in a secret civil ceremony in 1956 when the British Home Office denied continuance of her residency permit. In 1957, a bedside ceremony was performed in accordance with the Church of England, because they believed her death from bone cancer was imminent. However, her cancer went into remission, and she lived until 1960.

Till We Have Faces was published in 1956. It was Lewis' last novel, and he considered it to be his best, although the critics did not agree with him. The book used the mythological story of Psyche and Cupid as a vehicle to convey the everlasting and precious truths of the gospel.

C.S. Lewis left the Shadowlands of this world at 5:30 P.M. on November 22, 1963, the same day that President John F. Kennedy was assassinated in Dallas, TX. Although American history continues to be ambivalent concerning President Kennedy's impact, it can be said without the least hesitation that the influence of C.S. Lewis will turn minds and hearts to Christ well into the twenty-first century.

CHAPTERS 1-2

Eustace Clarence Scrubb is a lonely child whose parents have both spoiled him and turned him into an experiment to test their modern notions of child rearing. Hearing his cousins Lucy and Edmund were coming for a visit gives Eustace pleasure, not because he likes them, but because he enjoys bringing as much grief as possible into their lives. The children have to stay with their Aunt and Uncle for the summer because their parents are traveling to America and cannot afford to take them all. They are taking Susan and Peter is staying with Professor Kirke to study for a big exam.

Edmund and Lucy commiserate with each other over the misery they will have to endure with their cousin. As they sit together in Lucy's room, they reminisce about their adventures in Narnia, remembering that they had been told they would one day return. They are discussing a picture of what they believe is a Narnian ship.

In the midst of their discussion, Eustace enters and immediately begins an adversarial conversation with them about Narnia and the picture. When he asks what they like about the picture, Lucy replies it is how real it looks. All three of the children suddenly become aware that the waves in the picture are moving up and down, and they can feel the wind on their faces.

Eustace rushes toward the picture, declaring he will "smash the rotten thing." Edmund grabs him, telling him not to be a fool. Lucy holds onto the other side of Eustace, and they are drawn into the picture, finding themselves submerged in the water. Lucy is thankful for the hard work she invested into swimming lessons the summer before, but quickly discovers Eustace dragging her down .Edmund

comes to her rescue, along with a golden haired young man from the ship. Once they are onboard the ship, Lucy recognizes him as Caspian, who is a little older than she is.

Caspian is the king of Narnia. Caspian asks who their friend is, but Eustace is crying so loudly nothing else can be heard. Eustace loudly demands for Caspian to let him go. Caspian asks where he will go. Eustace rushes to the side of the ship as if expecting to see Lucy's bedroom, but is only greeted by the sea and the blue sky. He promptly becomes ill.

Caspian calls for Rynelf, one of the sailors, to bring spiced wine for their Majesties, because Lucy and Edmund have been previous rulers of Narnia. Eustace immediately grimaces and becomes ill again, demanding some Plumptree's Vitaminized Nerve Food with distilled water. He insists they put him ashore at the next opportunity.

When Reepicheep, the Chief Mouse and most valiant of all the Talking Beasts of Narnia, makes an appearance, Eustace is appalled. Lucy, on the other hand, is delighted. She wishes she could take him in her arms and hug him, but knows this will wound his dignity. Instead, she goes down on one knee before him. Reepicheep bows, twirls his whiskers and declares his loyalty to both Lucy and Edmund. Eustace restates his disgust at Reepicheep's presence. Reepicheep asks if Eustace is under the protection of Queen Lucy and King Edmund. He begins to say what he will do if Eustace is not when Lucy and Edmund both sneeze.

Caspian apologizes for leaving them standing there in wet clothing. He has them taken below where they are furnished with dry clothing. Since there are no females onboard, Lucy must wear some of Caspian's clothing. It is too large, but she can manage. The shoes are also too large, but she reasons she can go barefoot while on the ship. She feels very comfortable onboard the ship, since they often sailed when they were in Narnia previously. Lucy sighs contentedly, believing they are in for a lovely time.

Lucy rejoins Caspian, who introduces her to Lord Drinian, his captain. Edmund and Reepicheep are also present, but Eustace is not, and Edmund reports he is in bed. He advises they should leave him there since he only becomes worse if they are nice to him.

Edmund asks how much time has passed in Narnia since their last visit. It has been just over one year in England. Caspian informs them it has been three years; all is well in the kingdom; and peace reigns. He has set out on a quest to discover what became of the seven friends of his father's who were exiled by his Uncle Miraz when he usurped the throne from Caspian's father.

Reepicheep reveals he has an even higher goal – to sail to the far eastern end of the world and find Aslan's country. He recites a rhyme from his childhood that has driven him throughout his life.

Lucy asks about their voyage so far, and Captain Drinian brings them up to date. They have been at sea for nearly thirty days and will soon reach the Lone Islands. After that, they will be in uncharted waters.

Caspian suggests they tour the ship after supper. Lucy feels guilty about Eustace and remarks she could help him with his seasickness if she had her cordial. Caspian replies he brought it along, but asks if it should be wasted on seasickness. Lucy assures him it will only take a drop. Caspian leads them to a locker and withdraws Lucy's little diamond flask.

When they reach the cabin in which Eustace is lying, he asks when the storm will pass. The captain bursts out laughing, letting him know the weather is as fair as they will see. Lucy offers some of her cordial. He tells her to go away and leave him alone, but when she administers a drop, his normal color returns. He demands to be put ashore at the first port and announces he will "lodge a disposition" against them all with the British consul. Reepicheep asks what that is and how you lodge it, believing it to be a new kind of combat. Eustace can only say, "Imagine not knowing that."

They finally end up convincing Eustace they can no more send him to Cambridge than send him to the moon. Eustace reluctantly agrees to change into the clothing he has been given, and Caspian tours them through the ship. Although the Dawn Treader is a rather small ship, it is the largest vessel in the Narnian navy at this time, and Caspian's pride. As they tour, Eustace goes on about ocean liners, motor boats and airplanes, but Lucy and Edmund show unfeigned delight at everything they see. When they turn to the west and see the beauty of the sunset, feel the motion of the boat and taste the sea on their lips, Lucy feels too happy to speak.

As soon as Eustace has his clothing returned the next day, he begins to write in the little black notebook he always carries with him. He decides to use it as a diary now, writing about how horrible his circumstances are and particularly his feelings of disgust for Reepicheep. He mentions he will twist Reepicheep's tail the first opportunity he has.

Before dinner, things come to a head between Eustace and Reepicheep. Reepicheep is sitting on the bulwarks far forward on the ship, with his tail hanging down on the deck. This is one of his favorite places to sit, and the sailors enjoy his company. For some reason, Eustace makes his way this far forward on the ship, and grabs Reepicheep by the tail, beginning to spin him around.

Reepicheep, who is no stranger to fighting for his life, quickly draws his sword, jabs Eustace in the hand and lands on the deck facing Eustace. He challenges Eustace to draw his own sword, or he will beat him black and blue with the flat of his.

Eustace replies he is a pacifist and does not fight. He tells Reepicheep it was only a joke.

Reepicheep replies he will teach him how to respect a knight, and applies blows from the flat side of his sword to Eustace's bottom. Having never received a spanking before, Eustace covers the area to the cabin door in record speed. He can't believe how seriously everyone is taking it, with Caspian offering to loan him a sword and Drinian and Edmund discussing whether or not he should be handicapped in some way because of his size. He finally gives a sulky apology to Reepicheep, goes with Lucy to have his hand bandaged and lies down on his bunk (making sure he is on his side).

SUGGESTED ACTIVITIES CHAPTERS 1-2

1. The *Dawn Treader* is a sailing vessel designed like seagoing vessels of the middle ages, in which there were not only masts for sails, but also oars for rowing during periods when they faced calm winds. Have students research sailing vessels of this time period and draw their impression of the *Dawn Treader*.

2. If you live in an area where there is a naval museum, visit it and discuss the different types of ships.

3. Discuss Eustace's behavior. Why does he demand his own way in everything and bully Reepicheep? Will he change? How do others respond to him?

VOCABULARY CHAPTERS 1-2

teetotalers:	n	a person who abstains totally from intoxicating drink.
puny	adj	of less than normal size and strength; weak.
prow	n	the forepart of a ship or boat
gilded	adj	covered or highlighted with gold or something of a golden color.
listing	v	to incline to one side; career
assonance	n	the use of the same vowel sound with different consonants
roller	n	A long heavy wave of the sea, advancing toward the shore
briny	n	of or like brine; salty
endeavours	n	a strenuous effort; attempt.
vulgar	adj	marked by lack of taste, culture, delicacy, manners, etc
singularly	adv	unusual or strange; odd; different
discourteous	adj	showing bad manners; impolite; rude
exquisite	adj	extraordinarily fine or admirable
galley	n	the kitchen of a ship, boat, or aircraft
coronation	n	the act or ceremony of crowning a monarch
avenge	v	take revenge for or on behalf of
victual	n	food supplies; provisions.
leagues	n	a distance of about three miles
poop	n)	a superstructure at the stern of a vessel.
lodge	v	to bring a charge or accusation against someone
disposition	n	the final settlement of a matter
sulkily	adj	moody, surly, morose, churlish.
forecastle	n	the part of a vessel at the bow where the crew is quartered and stores, machines, etc, may be stowed
boatswain	n	an officer on a warship, or a petty officer on a merchant vessel, in charge of rigging, anchors, cables, etc.
cogs	n	a square-rigged, round-bottom boat used mainly for bulk trade
dromonds	n	large, fast-sailing ship of the Middle Ages
carracks	n	a merchant vessel having various rigs
galleons	n	a large sailing vessel of the 15th to the 17th centuries used as a fighting or merchant ship
usurper	n	one who seizes power without proper authority
ghastly	adj	terrifying; horrible
trice	n	a very short time; an instant
splayed	v	to spread out, expand, or extend
poltroon	n)	a wretched coward; craven.
pacifist	n	a person who is opposed to war or violence of any kind
rapier	n	a small sword, having a narrow blade and used for thrusting.
supple	adj	bending readily without breaking or becoming deformed
corporal	adj	of the human body; bodily; physical
novelty	n	the quality of being new and fresh and interesting

QUESTIONS CHAPTERS 1-2

1. Why does Eustace have no friends?

2. Proverbs 18:24 in the King James Version of the Bible says that, for a man to have friends, he must show himself friendly. How can you apply this to Eustace?

3. How does Eustace feel about his Pevensie cousins? Why is he glad Lucy and Edmund are coming?

4. Why are only Lucy and Edmund coming for the summer?

5. When Eustace makes up a rhyme about the children in Narnia, he says he uses assonance. What is assonance?

6. How are the children drawn into Narnia?

7. Who comes to help them out of the water?

8. Once they are on the ship, how does Eustace behave?

9. What causes Eustace to become most upset?

10. Contrast how Lucy is feeling about their adventure to Eustace's feelings.

11. What does Caspian reveal about the reason for this voyage?

12. What does Rheepicheep hope to achieve?

13. What problem do they encounter in Terebinthia?

14. What kind of ship do they encounter after leaving Terebinthia? What does Reepicheep think they should have done?

15. How is the ship powered when there is no wind to carry the sails?

16. What does Lucy use to help Eustace with his seasickness?

17. When Eustace speaks about "lodging a disposition," to what does Reepi chieep think he is referring?

18. What is Eustace's behavior like as they tour the ship?

19. What does Eustace do as soon as he receives his dried clothing the next morning?

20. How does the trouble between Eustace and Reepicheep come to a head? How is it settled?

ANSWERS TO QUESTIONS CHAPTERS 1-2

1. Eustace has no friends because he cares only for himself and what he wants; he demands that people give him what he wants all the time, and he loves to bully and boss people around.

2. Eustace is exactly the opposite of a friendly person. A friendly person cares about the other person before himself, while Eustace is always thinking only about himself. He doesn't try to be helpful or polite or gracious.

3. He does not like his Pevensie cousins and is jealous of their camaraderie that exists due to their experiences in Narnia. He is, however, glad Lucy and Edmund will be there for the summer so he can boss and bully them.

4. Their parents are going to America where their father has a job lecturing. Their mother and Susan are accompanying him. Peter is spending the summer with Professor Kirke studying for an exam, but he no longer lives in his large house and there is only room for Peter. Therefore, Lucy and Edmund are required to stay with their aunt and uncle.

5. Assonance is the repetition of vowel sounds when the consonants are not repeated.

6. Lucy and Edmund are admiring a painting in Lucy's room that has a ship which they identify as being Narnian. As they notice how realistic the painting is, Eustace becomes angry, wanting to destroy the painting. At the same time, Lucy and Edmund feel themselves being drawn into the picture. As Lucy enters the water, she feels Eustace dragging her down, then Edmund takes hold of him on the other side.

7. King Caspian

8. He is rude, angry, and belligerent; demanding that they immediately return him to Cambridge.

9. When Reepicheep enters and he sees a giant talking mouse, he becomes disgusted, voicing his hatred for mice in general and specifically what he considered to be "performing animals."

10. Eustace is miserable, complaining about everything, believing that every motion of the ship means they are in a storm. He finds fault with everything on the ship, and compares it to those of his time in Britain. By focusing on what is lacking, he makes himself more miserable. Lucy, on the other hand, is thrilled with everything and is looking forward to having a lovely adventure.

11. In order to seize power from Caspian's father, his uncle sent seven of his (Caspian's) father's friends away in ships. Now he is going on a quest to try to find them.

12. Reepicheep hopes to be able to find the far eastern end of the world and Aslan's land.

13. The people there are suffering from a sickness and they are not able to stop at the port city. They have to go around to a creek far from the city in order to take on water.

14. They run into pirates. Reepicheep thinks they should have "boarded her and hanged every mother's son of them."

15. Everyone but Reepicheep rows.

16. She uses a drop of her cordial after finding it is on board.

17. He thinks it is some form of warfare.

18. He continually makes remarks about the substandard quality of the ship and brings up ocean liners, motorboats, airplanes and submarines, which have no meaning whatsoever to the Narnians.

19. He begins keeping a diary, writing about how miserable he is and how horrible their circumstances are.

20. Eustace comes upon Reepicheep sitting on the bulwark, with his tail dragging on the deck for balance. Eustace grabs his tail and spins the mouse around. However, Reepicheep draws his sword and cuts Eustace's hand. The matter is settled when Eustace realizes Caspian and Edmund are discussing the possibility of having them settle it with a duel, and he apologizes to Reepicheep.

CHAPTERS 3-4

Early in the morning the first two of the Lonely Islands, Felimath and Doorn, are sighted. Lucy and Edmund's enthusiasm is immediately apparent, and Caspian asks if High King Peter conquered them. Edmund replies that they belonged to Narnia during the time of the White Witch. The author makes an aside to the effect that if he ever learns how they came under the control of the Narnian Crown, he will write the story. Drinian asks if they are going to land on Felimath. Edmund replies there will not be much good, since even during their time Felimath was virtually uninhabited. The people of Doorn and Arva only used Felimath for keeping sheep. Lucy expresses sorrow at not stopping at Felimath, saying it was lonely, but a good kind of loneliness. The groundcover was soft with grass and clover, and the sea air was also soft. Caspian adds that he would like to stretch his legs as well, so they decide they will go ashore, walk across the island and meet the *Dawn Treader* at the other end of the island. Caspian asks if Eustace cares to join them, and he retorts, "anything to get off this blasted boat."

So, Caspian, the two Pevensies, Reepicheep, and Eustace are rowed ashore and left on the island. They begin their trek, cresting a small hill from which they can look back at the *Dawn Treader* being rowed toward the northwest, and forward toward the island of Doorn. Doorn is separated from Felimath by a small channel. The island of Arva is further to the left. They can see the town of Narrowhaven on Doorn.

Suddenly Edmund spies six or seven armed, dangerous looking men. Caspian warns them not to reveal who they are. Reepicheep asks why. He replies they may not still acknowledge his rule, so they should not tip their hand until they have more swords. One of the men greets them and Caspian asks if there is still a governor over the islands. He informs them the governor's name is Gumpas, who is at Narrowhaven. He instructs the children to sit down and have a drink with them. Although they don't like the looks of the men, the children comply, Before they can realize what is happening to them, the children are disarmed and have their arms tied behind them. The men do not know what to make of Reepicheep, who is biting them as well as hurling insults at them. The leader warns the others not to harm him, since he will be worth the most money of the bunch.

Caspian remarks, "So that's what you are. Kidnappers and slavers." The leader tells him not to start complaining, since he has to make a living like anyone else. Lucy asks where he is taking them. He informs her he is taking them to Narrowhaven, where the market will take place the next day. Eustace inquires if there is a British Consul there, thoroughly confusing them with his jabbering.

The children are all tied together, but Reepicheep is separated. He continues to hurl insults at the men until Lucy wonders how any men could stand such things being said to them. On the contrary, the men are entertained, and encourage him to continue. They ask the children if one of them trained him and comment that he almost seems to know what he is saying. Reepicheep finally becomes so infuriated he falls silent.

They find a small village on the shore before crossing to Doorn, and the children see the slaver's bedraggled ship off shore. They are met by a nice looking bearded man who emerges from one of the houses and greets the slaver by name, calling him "Pug."

The man expresses an interest in buying Caspian, and asks the price. Pug gives him a price of three hundred crescents, but the man replies he will pay one hundred and fifty. The deal is made, and Lucy begins to beg they not be separated. She immediately stops, realizing that Caspian is not ready to be revealed.

As the others are taken away, Lucy is crying and Edmund looks blank. Caspian assures them it will all turn out well.

The man who has brought Caspian tells him he bought him for his face. He reminds him of his master, Caspian King of Narnia. Caspian reveals he is Caspian, the son of the Caspian this man remembers. The man asks how he can know it is true. Caspian replies that his face resembles his father's, and he has set out on a quest to seek the six men who were exiled by his Uncle Miraz, so he can guess who he is within six tries.

Lord Bern recognizes Caspian's resemblance to his father and immediately kneels down and swears allegiance to Caspian right there. Caspian asks about the allegiance of Gumpas, the current governor. Lord Bern advises Caspian that he should reveal himself with a show of power that is more than what he actually has. Lord Bern entertains them that night at his home in Arva, sending some of his men ahead to make arrangements. Caspian feels badly that the others are left in the hold of Pug's pirate ship, but that does not keep him from enjoying the company of Lord Bern and his daughters that evening.

The next morning Lord Bern advises his guests to dress in full battle regalia, polished until it will reflect the morning sun. They make their entry into Narrowhaven with the King's flag flying on his ship, and his trumpeter announcing his arrival. They are greeted by a crowd of people who have been alerted by Lord Bern the night before. Caspian steps on shore to shouts of, "Narnia, Narnia, Long live the King!" At the same moment, thanks to Bern's messengers, the bells begin ringing throughout the town.

As Caspian and his men advance, they draw their swords and march with their sternest faces. The sun reflecting off their armor shines brightly as they go. At first, they only have the people Bern alerted cheering them on. However, they quickly pick up the school children, the housewives and the young men and women. When they reach the gate of the castle where Gumpas sits in his slovenly way worrying about forms and rules and regulations, the entire town is stirred up and following them.

The guard meets them and mumbles that there are no interviews without appointments except between nine and ten PM the second Saturday of every month. Lord Bern quickly reprimands him for leaving his hat on in the presence of the King.

Before he understands what is happening, Caspian's men have the rusty gates open and are inside. They find the soldiers inside to be lounging casually, wiping their mouths and, for the most part, without armor and weapons.

Caspian, knowing they could be in a dangerous situation if the soldiers challenge them, decides to follow a strategy which will win the loyalty of the soldiers. He calls for the captain of the guard to stand before him. Telling the man he prefers his visit to be one of joy rather than terror, he informs him he will refrain from reprimanding him for the condition of their armor and weapons. He calls for a cask of wine to be brought out to drink to his health, and expresses his expectation of seeing them looking like men at arms with proper arms by noon the next day. Although the captain is left with his mouth gaping, Lord Bern calls for three cheers for the King, which changes the mood.

Caspian leaves the majority of his men in the courtyard, taking Bern and Drinian into the castle with him to confront Gumpas.

They find an obese man behind a desk who barely looks up when they enter. At first, he gives them the same canned speech about his availability.

Caspian nods to Bern. Bern and Drinian each take one end of the table, lift it and fling it to the other side of the room. They remove Gumpas from his chair and deposit him on the floor. Caspian sits on the floor, placing his unsheathed sword on his lap. Caspian begins by explaining he has not received the welcome he expected, then reveals himself as the King of Narnia.

Gumpas tries to back out by saying there was nothing about it in the correspondence or in the minutes. He had not been notified of it.

Caspian informs him he is there to inquire into Gumpas's conduct in office. He tells Gumpas they have not paid tribute to Narnia in one hundred and fifty years.

Gumpas begins to stall, saying he will have to talk to the council the next month; take up a report on the financial history of the islands at the first meeting the next year.

Caspian interrupts with a statement that the law allows that if the tribute is not delivered the entire amount will have to be paid by the Governor of the Lone Islands out of his private funds.

Gumpas begins to fumble for words, inwardly trying to scheme some way to rid himself of his unwanted visitors. Erroneously believing the King must have more than one ship, he is afraid he will never be able to outnumber the King's men.

Caspian goes on to speak to Gumpas of the slave trade he has been allowing to continue to flourish in the islands. Gumpas rationalizes that it is a necessary part of their economy. Caspian asks why they need slaves and Gumpas replies a great center of the trade. Caspian retorts that they are only lining the pockets of pirates like Pug. Gumpas speaks to Caspian as if he is a child, telling him he doesn't understand what the slave trade does for them. Caspian replies he knows it does not supply them with timber or food or the necessities of life.

Caspian informs Gumpas the slave trade must stop. Gumpas replies he cannot take responsibility for that. Caspian quickly tells him he is relieved of his office. Before Gumpas realizes what has happened, Caspian calls Bern to him and has him kneel. Bern is made a Duke; Duke of the Lone Islands.

Caspian forgives Gumpas the debt of the tribute, but tells him he needs to vacate the castle which now belongs to the Duke. One of Gumpas's secretaries makes a remark about them "playacting," but the Duke quickly lets them know they are very serious.

Caspian, Bern and Drinian immediately appropriate horses for themselves and rush to the slave market. Even Pug is left with his mouth ajar as they enter with their mail clanking and the Duke ordering them to their knees before the King. Those who don't obey are pulled down.

As Caspian stands before Pug, he informs the man he should lose his life for having laid hands on the King the day before. However, he will forgive him due to his ignorance. At the same time, he has forbidden slave trade in all his dominions.

He declares all the slaves in the market free. They all begin to cheer. Caspian asks for his friends. Lucy, Edmund and Reepicheep come forward. Those who bought them demand

a refund and Caspian orders Pug to return their money. Eustace has still not surfaced and Caspian asks about him. Pug replies with frustration that he could not find anyone who would take him, no matter how much he discounted the price. He orders one of his men to produce "Sulky" and Eustace is produced – still complaining.

They celebrate that night, then begin preparations the next day for the next leg of their journey. The *Dawn Treader* is worked over by the most skilled men on the islands, and Caspian speaks to anyone he can find who is an aged seaman, but no one has any knowledge of the eastern seas. Bern can only tell him his other companions sailed eastward.

As they prepare to leave, Bern tries to talk Caspian into staying. He replies that he has an oath to fulfill, and, beyond that, he would not know what to say to Reepicheep.

SUGGESTED ACTIVITIES CHAPTERS 3-4

1. Because this chapter deals with slavery, have students research various aspects of the history of slavery, and give presentations, then discuss how slavery has impacted different country's pasts.

2. Ask students to choose one of the main characters (other than Eustace) and write the events of this chapter as a journal entry from that character's point of view.

3. If students are mature enough to understand the current problem of children being sold, invite someone who is fighting against child slavery to speak to the students.

4. Have students compare/contrast the scene of Caspian with Gumpas and Jesus in the Temple with the money changers.

VOCABULARY CHAPTERS 3-4

remote	adj	out-of-the-way; secluded
uninhabited	adj	not lived in or on
turf	n	a layer of matted earth formed by grass and plant roots
consented	v	to permit, approve, or agree
writhing	v	to twist the body about, or squirm, as in pain
infuriated	v	to make furious; enrage.
suffocated	v	to smother
bedraggled	adj	limp and soiled, as with rain or dirt.
carrion	n	rottenness; anything vile
rigamarole	n	a set of incoherent or pointless statements; garbled nonsense
disbursed	v	to pay out money, especially for expenses; expend.
languishing	v	to be or become weak or feeble; droop; fade.
fief	n	a territory held in fee.
jetty	n	a landing pier; dock
postern	n	a back door or gate.
gauntleted	adj	wearing a mediaeval protective glove
dandified	adj	affecting extreme elegance in dress and manner
vagabonds	n	a carefree, worthless, or irresponsible person; rogue.
dossiers	n	a collection or file of documents on the same subject, especially a complete file containing detailed information about a person or topic.
consorts	n	one vessel or ship accompanying another.
abominable	adj	repugnantly hateful; detestable; loathsome
rabble	n	the lower classes; the common people
flogging	n	a beating administered with a whip or rod
galling	adj	irritating, exasperating, or bitterly humiliating
fortnight	n	a period of 14 consecutive days; two weeks
quest	n	an adventurous expedition undertaken by a knight to secure or achieve something

QUESTIONS CHAPTERS 3-4

1. When Caspian asks why the Lone Islands belong to Narnia, what is Edmund's answer?

2. When Lucy speaks of the grass and clover on Felimath, along with the soft sea air, what suggestion does Caspian make?

3. When they come upon seven rough looking men, why does Caspian warn them against revealing his true identity?

4. What is Reepicheep's solution to the situation?

5. How does Caspian respond to his idea?

6. When the men invite them to sit and drink with them, what happens?

7. What do they discover about the men?

8. What do the men think of Reepicheep?

9. To whom is Caspian sold?

10. Why is this ironic?

11. How does Caspian prove who he is?

12. What plan do they come up with to rescue the others?

13. Who meets them when they land at Narrowhaven?

14. What happens to the crowd as they go along?

15. Read Matt. 21:8-10; Matt27:20-25. How difficult is it for a mob to be persuaded to do something?

16. How does Caspian use his situation before the Governor's guard to his favor, earning him the loyalty of those troops?

17. What happens to Grumpas when he refuses to disband the slave trade?

18. How is Pug's reaction to Caspian different this time than the last time he saw him? Is it important how we dress?

19. What has Eustace become known as?

20. When Bern asks Caspian to stay and help in case there is war with Calorman, what is his reply?

ANSWERS TO QUESTIONS CHAPTERS 3-4

1. They belonged to Narnia during the time of the White Witch.

2. He suggests the *Dawn Treader* put them ashore and allow them to walk across the island while the ship skirts the island and picks them up on the other end.

3. He knows he will be a more valuable hostage if it is known he is the King of Narnia.

4. Reepicheep wants to draw his sword and defend Narnia.

5. Caspian reminds him they do not have the manpower to win a fight at this point and they do not want to do something foolhardy.

6. Before they can react, they are tied up and have been taken captive.

7. They are slavers.

8. They think he is some kind of a trained animal, rather than the talking animal of Narnia, and they are fascinated by him.

9. Lord Bern

10. This is one of the men he has been seeking.

11. Lord Bern immediately recognizes the similarity between Caspian and his father. Caspian uses that as the springboard to prove his case, explaining that when his uncle usurped the throne he exiled seven men and he is now on a quest to find those men, naming six of them. Bern recognizes the similarity of their face and voice and knows the story is true.

12. Bern suggests Caspian have his ship signal as if he has a fleet. Meanwhile, Bern sends word to his supporters to be ready to greet Caspian in the morning.

13. A small crowd of Bern's supporters greet them when they land, with great shouts of support for Narnia and the King.

14. They begin to collect more and more people as they move through the streets. People are attracted to the sounds of the celebration, close their shops and join in, celebrating the return of the King.

15. These Scriptures are excellent examples of cases of "mob mentality." When Jesus entered Jerusalem the mobs were there to lay down their garments and sing "Hosanna" and hail Him as king. However, just a few days later, the same crowds were persuaded to demand that he be crucified and Barabbas be released. People do not want to stand against the path of a crowd, but if there is a celebratory crowd that can be gathered, human nature desires to join it.

16. Because the troops are undisciplined and slovenly, he chastises them, then softens that blow by telling the captain he wants his return to be a time of celebration. He will give them a cask of wine to celebrate today, but expects them to be looking like men at arms by noon the next day or they will receive punishment.

17. He is removed from his position and Bern replaces him.

18. Pug is astounded when he sees Caspian.. The way a person is dressed does change the way people perceive them.

19. Sulky

20. "What would I tell Reepicheep?"

CHAPTERS 5-6

After *almost* three weeks on the Lone Islands, the time arrives for the departure of the *Dawn Treader*. All repairs have been made; Caspian has made his last speech; and the crowds have gathered to cheer them on their way. As they sail east, the first few days are idyllic, and Lucy feels she is the luckiest girl in the world. She passes the time playing chess with Reepicheep, who usually wins except when his mind wanders to real battles instead of focusing on the game. One evening everything changes when the weather suddenly turns deadly. Drinian orders Lucy below, and she immediately obeys him. The storm continues for several days – thirteen according to the journal Eustace is keeping. During the storm most of their food and water washes overboard and the mainmast is also broken. Once the storm ends the sea becomes becalmed and they have to decide whether to go forward or back. The decision is made to go forward, although Eustace is in disagreement.

Since water has to be rationed, Eustace feels he is suffering more than the others and tries to sneak extra water in the middle of the night only to be discovered by Reepicheep, much to his chagrin. Eustace is made to apologize to Reepicheep, which sends him to his bed for the rest of the day. Shortly after this episode, they sight land but are not able to go ashore until the next day according to Caspian's orders. This also causes Eustace to grumble against Caspian for not allowing them to go ashore sooner.

Once onshore everyone begins working to make repairs to the *Dawn Ttreader* except for Eustace, who climbs the side of the mountain in search of a place for a nap. As he climbs he is surrounded by a fog that causes him to feel the deepest loneliness he has ever felt in his life. He finally falls asleep only to awaken later feeling that he has slept much longer than he intended. He leaps up at a panic and tries to rush down the side of the mountain. Although he feels he's gone too far to the left, he continues down as fast as he can fearing that Caspian and the Pevensies may have left him. As the fog clears and Eustace reaches the bottom of the valley he suddenly realizes the sea cannot be seen.

At the same time the others are gathering for dinner and realize that Eustace is missing. Eustace looks around the narrow valley, realizing he's come down the wrong side of the mountain. He turns around to try to figure out how to get out of this Valley when he sees something moving in that cave. There are two thin wisps of smoke coming from the cave. Eustace knows nothing about dragons, so he doesn't know what he is facing. When the Dragon does show itself, it appears very old and sad. Eustace considers trying to escape but thinks he would not be able to. The Dragon, on the other hand, is so old it tries to make it to the pool to drink, but instead it lies down and dies. Eustace is quite relieved, until it starts to rain and he has to find shelter. Since the only shelter is the Dragon's Lair, that is where he goes for shelter. He becomes fascinated by the treasure that is there. He slips a diamond bracelet on his wrist, and falls asleep on top of the treasure. While the others are searching for him Eustace is sleeping. When he awakes he finds his arm terribly swollen. He does not understand the pain in his arm, but decides it must have swollen while he was asleep. He moves his right arm in front of him and in the moonlight sees a Dragon's claw. He decides it is the Dragon's mate. Looking to his left, he sees a claw there, too. Eustace begins to cry. When he cries huge tears splash down on the treasure in front of him. As he tries to crawl from between the two dragons, he inches out to the pool where he sees his reflection and realizes he has been turned into a dragon himself. His first thoughts are that he can get even with Caspian and Edmund. Then he realizes he doesn't want to; he wants to be friends. He wants to be back with humans. He would even be happy for a kind word from Reepicheep. He realizes that Caspian would never have sailed away and left him. Caspian has too much integrity for that. The others have been looking for Eustace and have seen the dragon in the valley. They have been concerned that perhaps the dragon has eaten Eustace. Then, during the night, a dragon is seen flying above them in the sky. In the morning the dragon is seen at the beach. They don't know what to make of the tears coming from its eyes. As they question it, Lucy notices the swollen foreleg and tries to cure it with her cordial. Not only does it not work, but Caspian recognizes the bracelet and is clearly concerned.

SUGGESTED ACTIVITIES CHAPTERS 5-6

1. Have a meteorologist visit the class and explain the damages the hurricane would cause to the kind of sea vessel the children were traveling in.

2. Have students draw a map of the island on which they have landed showing the mountain on which Eustace got lost in the valley in which he found the Dragon.

3. Have students write a story about forgiveness, either something that has actually happened to them or something that they make up which illustrates the fact that forgiveness is a requirement for the person who is doing the forgiving more than the person who is being forgiven.

VOCABULARY CHAPTERS 5-6

Prow	n	the forepart of a ship or boat; bow.
Buskins	n	a thick-soled, laced boot or half boot.
Jerkins	n	a close fitting jacket or short coat, usually sleeveless as one of leather worn in the 16th and 17th centuries
Forlorn	adj	lonely and sad; forsaken.
Sinister	adj	bad, evil, base, or wicked;
Battened	v	to cover (a hatch) so as to make watertight
Reef	v	to shorten (sail) by tying in one or more reefs.
Cataract	n	a descent of water over a steep surface
Listing	v	to cause (a vessel) to incline to one side
Appalling	adj	causing dismay or horror
Embarked	v	to board a ship, aircraft, or other vehicle, as for a journey
wireless	n	*Chiefly British* , radio.
Fiends	n	a diabolically cruel or wicked person.
Prig	n	a person who is smugly and self-righteously narrowminded
patronizing	adj	having a superior manner; condescending
odious	adj	highly offensive; repugnant; disgusting.
Fjord	n	a long, narrow arm of the sea bordered by steep cliffs
Oppressive	adj	burdensome, unjustly harsh, or tyrannical
Blighter	n	a contemptible, worthless person
Precipices	n	a cliff with a vertical, nearly vertical, or overhanging face
slewed	v	to turn, swing, twist,
lithe	adj	bending readily; pliant; limber; supple; flexible
shamming	v	to make a false show of something; pretend
stealthily	adv	characterized by great caution, secrecy, etc; furtive
hoard	n	a supply or accumulation that is hidden or carefully guarded for preservation
disquieting	adj	causing anxiety or uneasiness; disturbing

QUESTIONS CHAPTERS 5 - 6

1. How long did the Dawn Treader stay in the Lone Islands?

2. How did Lucy describe the weather when they first left?

3. What metaphor and simile does Lucy use to describe the sea and the sky as the hurricane begins to take place?

4. As Lucy describes the storm she uses another metaphor to describe the storm. What is it?

5. According to Eustace, how long does the hurricane continue?

6. Once the storm is over what are the difficulties they face?

7. What happens to Eustace when he tries to get extra water in the night?

8. What are the consequences of his actions? How does this make Eustace feel?

9. When they land on an island, why does Eustace not go where everyone else is?

10. How does Eustace show that he's changed even as he tries to get out of work with the others?

11. When Eustace made it to the top of the mountain and lay down to enjoy himself why does he find that he cannot enjoy himself?

12. Read Proverbs 6:10,, Proverbs 10:5, Proverbs 20:13, and 2 Thessalonians 3:11-12.. According to the Scriptures, what actions of Eustace have been set into play to cause him to suffer consequences for his actions? Be specific.

13. When Eustace finds himself in the Valley what does he discover?

14. When Eustace takes shelter in the dragon's lair what is the first thing that he finds there?

15. According to first Timothy 6:10, the love of money is what? How does this play out in Eustace's life?

16. When Eustace first realizes that he's a dragon what is his first desire?

17. What does he immediately realize?

18. Read Proverbs 20:22, Proverbs 24:29, Matthew 7:12, Romans 12:17, first Peter 3:9, and relate how these Scriptures explain how Eustace is feeling.

19. When Eustace comes to the others who realizes that he is crying?

20. When Lucy tries to take down the swelling with her magic cordial what happens to the dragon's paw?

ANSWERS TO QUESTIONS CHAPTERS 5 – 6

1. three weeks.

2. Lucy says the next few days are delightful. She thinks she is the most fortunate girl in the world. She can see reflections of the sunlit water dancing on the ceiling of her cabin every morning.

3. The metaphor Lucy uses is that the clouds build up a rack that suddenly have a gap torn in them. The simile she uses is that the sea was a drab or yellowish color like dirty canvas.

4. The next metaphor that Lucy uses to describe the storm is that a great hill of water rushes to meet them that looks like certain death and that they were tossed on top of it.

5. 13 days.

6. The mast is broken, much of their food has been swept overboard, their water casks have also been swept overboard leaving them short on water; they have lost their chickens, and they were becalmed.

7. He is caught by Reepicheep.

8. He has to apologize to Reepicheep, and Caspian makes it clear that anyone else found stealing water will get two dozen lashes.

9. Everyone else is working to restore the ship. Eustace decides he wants to find a place where he can be alone and take a nap.

10. As he climbs the mountain to find a place to be alone Eustace keeps going even past the place where he would've given up before he came on this adventure.

11. He suddenly finds himself feeling so lonely that he's uncomfortable. He finds that the loneliness is not what he wants to feel. He thought he wanted to be alone but being alone just causes him and achiness.

12. God has commanded that we should not be slothful or lazy. All of the other members of the crew aboard the ship are working to restore the ship so that they can set sail again. Eustace should be working with them. Instead he is choosing to be lazy. Laziness is never God's will. Because he is choosing this action he will have to suffer the consequences of that action.

13. Instead of going back down the side of the mountain he had come up, he finds himself in a valley he had not been in before. He does not recognize where he is and he can't find the sea.

14. He finds the dragon's treasure.

15. The love of money is the root of all evil. In Eustace's case he is drawn to the dragon's treasure, and is turned into a dragon.

16. His immediate desire is to get even with Edmund and Caspian.

17. He immediately realizes that he does not want to get even with them; he wants to be friends with them.

18. These Scriptures all refer to the fact that God does not want us to repay evil for evil. Even when someone has done bad things to us we need to pray for them and not try to get back at them. Eustace began to realize that. His desire was not to get even with Edmund and Caspian but try to be friends with them.

19. Lucy

20. Eustace hopes that the cordial would turn him back into a boy. However, it does help his arm some, but it's not able to take the swelling down all the way and he is still a dragon.

CHAPTERS 7-8

Caspian points out that the bracelet on the Dragon had once belonged to the Lord Octesian. Reepicheep asks if the dragon has eaten the Narnian lord. Lucy suggests that Octesian was turned into the dragon. Edmund adds that although neither choice may be correct they can safely assume Octesian did not get any further than this island. Through questioning the dragon they finally discover that the dragon is Eustace. When they realize how upset Eustace is they all try to comfort him. For the first time in his life Eustace begins to understand what it is to have friends. He tries to communicate with them what happened, but is unsuccessful. He helps the others by bringing them food, flying over the island and bringing back a pine tree for the mast, as well as providing warmth for them at night when they're sleeping. One of the developments during this time that changes Eustace's outlook is that Reepicheep becomes one of his most kindly and constant companions. Reepicheep tries to point out to him examples of famous men who have fallen from prosperity into desperate circumstances **yet** have nevertheless recovered and lived happily afterwards.

The question that is plaguing everyone is what to do with Eustace when the time comes for their voyage to continue. They don't know if he can fly along above them, if they can tow him behind, or if he could possibly make it on the deck of the *Dawn Treader*. Eustace realizes he has been a problem from the beginning and now he has become more of a problem than ever. This situation nags at his conscience just as the bracelet has been eating at his arm.

Edmund awakens early one morning to the sound of a voice and the sight of a body near him that is too large for Lucy and too small for Caspian. He goes to investigate and discovers that Eustace has been restored to his original body. Eustace invites Edmund to come with

him and he'll explain how his body has been restored to that of a boy. He tells Edmund how he was lying awake and a great lion came to him and told him to follow him. The lion brought him to a well and told him he was to undress and bathe in the well. Eustace questioned this since he had no clothes on. He then realized that dragons, like snakes, could probably shed their skins. He began to shed his skin. After three attempts to shed the skin himself the lion told him to lie down and he would remove his clothes for him. Eustace describes how it worked when the lion peeled the skin off. There was pain but at the same time there was a pleasure in the way it felt. The lion then grabbed and threw him into the water. Eustace found that all the pain was gone from his arm. He realized that the reason for that was that he was once again a boy. He describes his delight at seeing his own arms once again even though they might not be as muscular as Caspian's. The lion then took him out of the water and dressed him. Edmund explains to Eustace that he has had an encounter with Aslan. Eustace apologizes for his behavior since they have come on the *Dawn Treader*. Edmund explains that when he first came to Narnia he was a traitor. Eustace asks who Aslan is. Edmund explains that he is the great Lion, the son of the Emperor over the sea, who saved Edmund and saves Narnian. They are sailing toward Aslan's country

There is great rejoicing when the others discover that Eustace has been returned to a boy. They each have different theories about what happened to Octesian and no one wants his bracelet. Before they leave the island, Caspian has a commemoration carved into the cliff by the Bay. The bracelet is thrown up into the air and lands on a projection which is at a place where no one can reach it.

The next area they visit is one they have seen while flying over it when Eustace was a dragon. The area is deserted but there are some ruins. Caspian believes the ruins to be the work of Pirates, but Edmund thinks possibly it was the dragon's work. They do find a small boat made of hide stretched over wicker that looks like it was made for a child. Reepicheep decides to keep it for himself and they sail on. After five days of good weather they have a day of rain and Eustace loses two games of chess to Reepicheep. Edmund mentions that he wishes he were in America with Susan. Suddenly Lucy spies something out of window. They find themselves attacked by a sea monster. Although Eustace bravely tries to attack it with one of Caspian's old swords, they find they have to push it away from the ship to keep it from trying to squeeze the ship to bits. It is Reepicheep who comes up with the order to not fight but to push.

After surviving the attack by the sea serpent, they sail for three days with clear skies. On the fourth day the wind changes in the afternoon and they are facing gale force winds. However, they sight land and steer into a natural harbor at night, waiting until the next morning to go ashore. Because their water casks need to be replenished they need to seek out the streams to fill them. There are two streams available, and Drinian prefers the eastern stream which is closer, but Edmund chooses the other stream which provides more shelter from the rain. Caspian votes with Edmund and that is the choice they make. When the rain is over Caspian, Eustace, the Pevensies, and Reepicheep decide to walk to the top of the hill and see what they can see. As they explore the island they begin to move toward the other stream. They find a small mountain lake surrounded by cliffs. Everyone sits down except Edmund who jumps up. He discovers he has sat on the edge of an ancient sword. As they investigate, they realize it is a Narnian sword. They also find a helmet, a dagger, some Narnian coins, and the

remains of a mail shirt. This leads them to conclude one of the Narnian lords must have been on this island. The question is what happened to him? They come to an opening where the stream comes out of the lake and there is a pool. Eustace comes very close to stooping down and taking a drink of water. They notice a golden statue deep in the water and Caspian wonders if they can get it out. Reepicheep suggests they can dive for it. Edmund tries to determine the depth of the water with his hunting spear. However, Lucy tells him the statue must not be gold because his spear now also appears to be gold. Edmund replies that his spear has suddenly become very heavy. Edmund is also having trouble with his boots and orders everyone to get back from the water. He announces that the water is turning everything into gold. It has turned the spear into gold and has turned the toes of his boots into gold. They surmise that the statue is not a statue at all but the missing Narnian lord. They realize what a narrow escape they've all had. Caspian announces that the king who owns this island would be the richest king and all the world. He claims it as a Narnian possession. He names it Goldwater island. He binds them all to secrecy, telling them that they should not reveal it to anyone on pain of death. Edmund takes offense, telling Caspian that he is under allegiance to him and to the high King his brother. Lucy tells them to stop it and suddenly they see the figure of Aslan. He is gone as quickly as he came but they all realize that they should not be arguing and that this place has had an effect on them. Reepicheep suggests they name the island Deathwater. When they returned to the ship Drinian mentions that the Kings and Queens all seem to be bewitched. The only thing they disclose is that they found the body of one of the lords they were looking for. Rhince replies that they have found three; there are only four more to go. Maybe they'll be home after the new year.

SUGGESTED ACTIVITIES CHAPTERS 7-8

1. Because of the fact that Eustace experiences salvation at this time. This would be a good time to bring in a pastor or youth pastor to talk with students about salvation.

2. When Eustace realizes how difficult his actions have been, and how much discomfort he's caused for everyone else, he apologizes for his actions. Ask students to write a note of apology to someone they think they might have offended at some time by their actions.

3. Ask students choose one of the characters and write a journal entry from the perspective of that character.

4. Discuss with students the things Eustace gained by being a dragon and the things he lost. Ask them to determine whether they feel he lost more or gain more by being dragon.

5. Ask students to draw a map of the island, marking the important places to the story.

VOCABULARY CHAPTERS 7-8

ejaculations	n	an abrupt, exclamatory utterance
unmitigated	adj	unqualified or absolute
relapses	n	an act of falling back into a former state or practice
coracle	n	a small roundish boat made of skins stretched on a wicker frame
vermilions	n	a brilliant red
valor	n	boldness or determination when facing danger
baccy	n	an informal name for tobacco

QUESTIONS CHAPTERS 7-8

1. When they first see the bracelet on the dragon's arm, to whom do they realize it belongs?

2. Once they realized the dragon is Eustace, how do they feel he has changed?

3. How is Eustace able to help everybody in his dragon form?

4. What is the only thing that keeps Eustace from despair during this time?

5. Who becomes the closest comforter to Eustace during this time? Why is this ironic?

6. As time goes by what is the problem facing everyone, and how does this affect Eustace?

7. When Eustace becomes a boy again who is the first person with whom he shares his experience? Why is this choice particularly important?

8. Who comes to Eustace during the night? What instructions does he give him?

9. As Eustace attempts to remove the dragon scales himself what does he discover? How are they finally removed?

10. Look at Ephesians 2: 8-10. What does this say about salvation? How does this compare to what Eustace experienced?

11. After this what does Aslan do for him?

12. Look at 2 Cor 5:17, Isaiah 61:10, and Revelation 7:9. How can you compare these verses to what Eustace experienced?

13. When Eustace apologizes to Edmund for his bad behavior what does Edmund reveal about himself to Eustace?

14. What does Caspian decide to do in honor of Octesian? What becomes of the bracelet?

15. What is the next danger they face on the sea? How does Eustace display his valor?

16. What wisdom does Reepicheep have that saves them?

17. When they arrive at the next island and they are deciding which stream to choose, what simile does Lewis use to describe the way Drinian is steering the boat?

18. As they explore the island after filling the casks with water what do they discover?

19. What do they find at the bottom of the pool and how does this affect them?

20. Read 1 Timothy 6:10. How does this verse relate to the behavior of Caspian and Edmund after they discover the gold on the island?

ANSWERS TO QUESTIONS CHAPTERS 7-8

1. Octesian

2. They no longer feel he is so annoying. They see that he is trying to help them and they feel sorry for him because he is trapped in the dragon's body.

3. He is able to bring them animals for food, he keeps them warm at night, he flies over the island so that they can see the lay of the land, and he brings them a tree for the mast.

4. For the first time in his life he has friends.

5. Reepicheep. This is ironic because up until this point Eustace and Reepicheep have been the worst of enemies. Eustace could not find it in his heart to accept Reepicheep under any circumstances and yet Reepicheep goes out of his way to make life more bearable for Eustace as a dragon. In other words, Reepicheep is the "bigger man."

6. The problem they face is what they're going to do with Eustace when they leave the island. They are not sure how they can sail with a dragon in tow. This causes great concern for Eustace. He knows that he has been a problem for the whole voyage and now he's causing even more of a problem.

7. Edmund. This is particularly important because of the position Edmund was in on his first visit to Narnia.

8. Aslan comes to Eustace in the night. He tells Eustace to follow him until they come to a well. He then instructs Eustace to remove his clothing. Since Eustace has no clothing he assumes he supposed to remove his skin.

9. After three attempts Eustace discovers he is not able to remove the dragon skin on his own. It is only able to be removed when he submits himself to Aslan.

10. Ephesians 2:8 – 10 states that we are saved by grace through faith and not by works of our own. It is the work of Christ on the cross that saves us, not anything that we can do ourselves. What happened to Eustace is an illustration of this truth. He was not able by his own work to remove the dragon skin from himself. Only Aslan, who is a type of Christ, was able to remove the skin from him.

11. He made him a new creature by cleansing him in the well and then he clothed him with new clothing.

12. These verses say that we are made new creatures in Christ and that God clothes us in robes of righteousness. The scene that takes place with Eustace is a picture of this. Eustace becomes a new creature. He is a totally new boy. And he is clothed in new clothes by Aslan.

13. Edmund tells Eustace that on his first visit to Narnia he was a traitor.

14. Caspian has s sign carved into the side of a cliff in honor of Lord Octesian so that he won't be forgotten. The bracelet is thrown into the air and is catches on a projection where no one can reach it.

15. The next danger they face is a sea serpent. Eustace displays valor by trying to attack the sea serpent with a sword.

16. Reepicheep saves them by telling them not to fight but to push the sea serpent off the boat.

17. Lewis says that Drinian is steering the boat "like tiresome people in cars who continue at 40 miles an hour while you are explaining to them that they are on the wrong road."

18. They find armor, a dagger, some coins, and a shirt of mail that are definitely from Narnia.

19. At the bottom of the pool they find what they first think is a golden statue. They soon begin to argue over who has control over the island.

20. 1 Timothy 6:10 states that the love of money is the root of all evil. They find that this is true as they begin arguing with each other over the gold on this island. The pool turns things to gold but, in the end it's a curse. The statue at the bottom of the pool is not a statue but one of the Narnian lords they're looking for.

<u>CHAPTERS 9-10</u>

The winds begin to shift from a northwesterly direction to due west. They are now sailing straight into the rising sun. There is a dispute among those on board as to whether or not the sun is larger than it looked in Narnia. Just as it seems they are sailing on a sea that is endless and their stores are becoming depleted, they sight land. This land seems strange indeed. Although it appears uninhabited, the lawns and grass are well-kept, smooth and short. Other than the sounds of pigeons cooing the place is eerily silent. They find a long straight path that leads to a house. As soon as they step on to the path, Lucy gets a stone in her shoe. When she stops to remove it, she become separated from the others. Getting her shoe back on, she realizes she can no longer hear the others, but she hears a thumping sound followed by disembodied voices. When the voices stop and the thumping begins again Lucy runs to warn the others.

Meanwhile, the others have reached the house. Eustace declares the place deserted, but Caspian points out the smoke rising from the chimney. They enter a gated courtyard and find a water pump pumping itself. Lucy arrives and tells them of her experience. They move back to the beach, concerned about what will happen to them if they become involved in a battle against invisible foes and those on the *Dawn Treader* won't know how to interpret it.

They are soon joined by a group of disembodied voices who threaten them if they do not cooperate. The voices explain to them that they need Lucy to perform a courageous act in order to remove a spell from them so they will no longer be invisible. At first those with Caspian tell the voices they will not agree to allow Lucy to carry out such a risky mission. However, Lucy convinces them that it is the only way to save all of them. Because evening is falling, the voices invite them to an evening meal. They are amused as they watch the dishes moving up and down towards the table. They wonder what kind of creatures these are.

The voices have told them there is a magician on the island that turned them all invisible. Only a young girl who reads the spell from the magician's book will be able to turn them visible again. Lucy starts upstairs in the morning armed with the instructions she has been given. She follows the directions very carefully, coming to the appointed room and finding that she cannot close the door behind her. She immediately recognizes the book in the center of the room on a stand. She begins to look through the book and is fascinated with what she sees.

At one point she sees a spell that would make her beautiful beyond the lot of mortals. Lucy sees herself on the page at this point more beautiful than she could ever imagine. She sees Susan as being jealous of her because of her beauty and she decides she's going to say the spell. Just as she begins to say the spell the face of Aslan stares into hers. He is angry. She becomes afraid and turns the page. On another page she finds a spell to know how other people think of her. She recites the words and sees a vision of two of her friends talking about her. She hears one of her friends who was close to her saying things that are unflattering and she becomes hurt. Next she comes to a spell for the refreshment of the spirit and there is a beautiful story which goes on for several pages. Lucy reads the story and for years she tries to remember it but she never can. She only remembers that it's a beautiful story. She continues to turn the pages and finds a page with no pictures. The first words are a spell to make things visible. She reads through it to make sure that she can pronounce the hard words and then begins to say it out loud. As she speaks the words the colors on the page begin to become visible. It has the appearance of invisible writing suddenly becoming visible except that this is much more colorful and beautiful. Suddenly she hears soft heavy footfalls behind her. Turning, she sees Aslan behind her. She tells him that it is kind of him to come. He replies that he was there all along, but her words have made him visible. She scoffs at this, saying surely nothing she could do would make him visible. Aslan asks her if she doesn't think he would have to obey his own rules.

After a pause Aslan speaks again. He brings up the issue of her eavesdropping. He tells her she was listening to two of her school friends. She replies that she didn't think it was really eavesdropping because it was magic. He tells her it is still eavesdropping even if it is magic and she has misjudged her friend. Her friend loves her very much but she was afraid of the older girl and said things that she didn't mean. Lucy asks Aslan if she has spoiled their relationship for good. Aslan replies that he has told her before that he will never tell her what would have happened. Then she asks him if she could please

read the beautiful story again. He replies that he will tell it to her again for years and years, but now he wants to take her to meet the master of the house.

SUGGESTED ACTIVITIES CHAPTERS 9-10

1. Ask students to write a story about being invisible. What would it feel like? How would they use the cloak of invisibility?

2. Have a discussion about the two spells that tempted Lucy and how she handled them. If Aslan had not appeared would she have gone through with the spell to make herself unbelievably beautiful? How would that have changed her?

3. Divide students into groups and have them write skits depicting different scenes from these chapters and perform them.

<u>VOCABULARY CHAPTERS 9-10</u>

extracted	v	to get, pull, or draw out, usually with special effort, skill, or force
mallets	n	a hammer like tool with a head commonly of wood
dreadful	adj	causing great dread, fear, or terror
conspicuous	adj.	Easily seen or noticed; readily visible
folly	n	the state or quality of being foolish
parley	v	to hold an informal conference with an enemy under a truce
skulking	v	to move in a stealthy manner; slink
enmity	n	a feeling or condition of hostility; hatred; ill will
proposal	n	the act of offering or suggesting something for acceptance
downright	adj	absolute; frankly direct; straightforward
deceive	v	to mislead by a false appearance or statement; delude
muck	n	filth, dirt, or slime
reckoned	v	to count, compute, or calculate
flagged	adj	descriptive of any hard stone that splits and is suitable for paving
treacherous	adj	characterized by faithlessness or readiness to betray trust; traitorous
inquisitive	adj	given to inquiry, research, or asking questions, eager for knowledge
keen	adj	eager; interested; enthusiastic
victuals	n	food supplies; provisions
mead	n	an alcoholic liquor made by fermenting honey and water
grimace	n	a facial expression, often ugly or contorted, that indicates disapproval, pain, etc.
infallible	adj	absolutely trustworthy or sure
muddlesome	adj	to mix things together in a confused or disordered way
fury	n	unrestrained or violent anger, rage, passion, or the like
mortals	n	of or pertaining to human beings as subject to death; human
corridor	n	a gallery or passage connecting parts of a building; hallway
eavesdropping	v	to listen secretly to a private conversation

QUESTIONS CHAPTERS 9-10

1. What change takes place that is totally different from what they have experienced before?

2. What causes a disagreement among the people aboard?

3. When they land on the new island what seems odd about it?

4. When Lucy falls behind to remove a stone from her shoe what does she experience?

5. When Eustace thinks the house is empty what evidence does Caspian point out that someone must be there?

6. What advice does Reepicheep give them about trying to avoid an invisible army?

7. What do the voices tell them they want? Why?

8. What is Lucy's reasoning for deciding to accept the task that the invisible voices asked her to do?

9. What is Reepicheep's response?

10. How does Lewis describe the service at the feast when they are served by the invisible voices?

11. When Eustace is talking to Edmund what creatures does he bring up that he thinks these people might be like?

12. What two similes does Lewis use to explain how Lucy felt on the morning when she woke up?

13. As Lucy goes up the stairs she can hear something, but after the first flight she can no longer hear it. What is it, and what does that indicate?

14. What is the first thing Lucy sees that frightens her?

15. When Lucy finds the room with the book, what does she find unpleasant about it?

16. What is the first spell that tempts Lucy? What stops her?

17. Look at Prov. 31:30, Psalm 149:4, 1Pet. 3:4, and 2 Cor. 3:18. What do these verses have say in relationship to the way Lucy is feeling as she is tempted to cast the spell that would make her more beautiful than any other mortal?

18. Taking into consideration the verses in the previous question why does Aslan stop her?

19. What happens when Lucy does cast the spell that allows her to eavesdrop on her friends? How does that make her feel?

20. When Lucy finds the spell to make hidden things visible, who shows up?

21. What does Aslan tell her when Lucy says she doesn't think she could have made him visible?

22. Why does Lucy think her eavesdropping was not wrong? What does Aslan tell her?

23. When Lucy asks if she has spoiled everything what is Aslan's response?

24. What does Lucy want Aslan to allow her hear again?

25. Who does Aslan tell Lucy he's going to introduce her to?

ANSWERS TO QUESTIONS CHAPTERS 9-10

1. The winds change from a Northwest direction to due West.

2. Some think the sun looks larger than it looked in Narnia and others disagree.

3. Everything about the land gives the appearance that it is well-kept. The grass is smooth and short as if gardeners have cut the grass; the trees are separated; there are no broken branches; there are no leaves lying on the ground; but the entire island is silent with the exception of the cooing pigeons. They can find no evidence of people anywhere.

4. At first she hears thumping sounds then she hears a voice. After that she hears several voices. The voices indicate they are going to cut the group off from their ship and capture them.

5. There is smoke rising from the chimney.

6. There is no way to avoid an invisible enemy by creeping and skulking. Reepicheep says he would rather face them in battle face-to-face than to be caught by the tail.

7. They want Lucy to go upstairs in the house and read from the magic book in order to cast the spell over them so that they will no longer be invisible. It is necessary for a little girl to read the spell from the book. They are afraid for any of their little girls to go upstairs and so they have been waiting for someone with a little girl the right age to land on the island and convince her to go upstairs and do this for them.

8. Lucy chooses to do the task because she considers the people to be not very brave and not very clever, but at the same time she wants to save her life and the lives of those who are with her. She sees no other way they can avoid being chopped to bits by this group.

9. Reepicheep agrees with Lucy. He says that if there was any insurance they could save her in a battle it would be their duty to do so, but he sees none.

10. The food progresses up the dining hall in a series of bounds or jumps. The highest point of each jump a dish would be about 15 feet up in the air. Then it would come down and stop quite suddenly about 3 feet from the floor. With a dish containing anything like soup the result was rather disastrous.

11. Huge grasshoppers or giant frogs

12. like waking up on the day of an examination or day when you are going to the dentist

13. She hears the ticking of the clock, but can no longer hear it after the first flight of stairs. This is an indication that time has no effect from this point on.

14. She sees herself in a mirror that makes her look like a magician with a beard and hair on the top.

15. She finds it unpleasant that she cannot close the door. She must stand reading the book with her back to the door.

16. It is a spell that would make her more beautiful than any mortal. She is stopped by the face of Aslan showing his teeth.

17. These verses indicate that what is important to God is not outward beauty but the beauty that comes from within. Lucy is tempted because she wants to be more beautiful than her sister Susan and this is wrong. She should not be comparing herself to Susan, but trying to become more like Christ. Only when we become Christlike can we please God.

18. Aslan stops her because he knows that to go through with that spell would be destructive to Lucy.

19. She hears her friends talking and one of her friends says something that is hurtful to her. This cuts are very deeply.

20. Aslan

21. He tells her that he has to obey his own rules

22. She thinks it was not wrong because it is magic. Aslan tells her that spying on people by magic is the same as spying on them any other way, and she has misjudged her friend.

23. He tells her that no one's ever told what would have happened.

24. She wants to be able to read the story again that was for the refreshment of the spirit in the pages of the book. Aslan tells her he will tell it To Her for years and years.

25. Aslan tells her he's going to introduce her to the master of the house.

CHAPTERS 11-12

Lucy follows Aslan into the passage where they are met by an old man with a long white beard wearing a red robe. He is barefoot and sports a crown of oak leaves. He is leaning on a carved staff. The man bows before Aslan and welcomes him. Aslan asks Coriakin if he has grown weary of ruling the foolish subjects Aslan has given him. Coriakin replies that they are very stupid but harmless. He is looking forward to the day he will be able to rule them with wisdom instead of magic. Coriakin asks Aslan if he will show himself to the people. With a half growled that Lucy interprets as a laugh, Aslan replies that they are not ready yet and he would frighten them out of their senses.

He tells them he is going to Trumpkin the Dwarf in Cair Paravel. He will tell Trumpkin Lucy's story. He tells Lucy not to look so sad, that he will see her again soon. He is immediately gone, leaving Lucy and Coriakin alone. The magician asks if she is hungry and provides a meal for Lucy while he eats bread and wine.

Afterward Lucy asks Coriakin if he will take away the spell of ugliness as well. Coriakin explains they are not actually that ugly, but the Chief Duffer believes they are, and the others believe everything he says. Lucy asks why the spell was put on them to begin with. Coriakin explains that their job is to tend the garden and he had asked them to take water from a stream that runs right by the garden instead of going half a mile to a spring. They refused. Lucy asks if they are really that stupid. Coriakin gives her several examples of outrageous behavior. Coriakin sees Lucy is finished and suggests they go to another room where she will be able to see the Duffers. At first she only sees what she thinks are mushrooms. They begin to wake up and she realizes they are monopods – beings with only one large leg and one enormous foot. They move by jumping on their gigantic foot. Lucy inquires what they were before and Coriakin replies they were dwarves. Lucy tells him they are so funny it

would be a shame to turn them back. Coriakin convinces Lucy it is up to her to assure the Duffers that they are not ugly. She runs down the steps, barreling into Edmund at the bottom of the steps. She vouches for the magician and tells them she has seen Aslan. She quickly goes to the Duffers who celebrate her for lifting the spell of invisibility. Lucy sways their opinions of themselves, telling them they are very nice looking. Caspian and the Narnians go to the *Dawn Treader* to give the news to Rhince. The Duffers make so much noise that Eustace says he wishes the magician had made them inaudible instead of invisible. He is soon sorry when he tries to explain this.

Reepicheep gets out his little boat and shows the Duffers how to use their foot as a raft. Soon they are paddling around the harbor like a fleet of canoes. They combine their new name of monopods with Duffers and come up with Dufflepuds.

The Narnians dine with the magician that evening. Each person has their favorite dish to eat. After the meal Coriakin has Drinian describe their travels while he magically draws a map of their voyages. They conclude the golden man in Deathwater was Lord Restimar. The next day the magician mends the stern that was damaged by the sea serpent.

After leaving the island of the Dufflepuds they sail for 12 days without sighting land. On the 13th day Edmund sights what appears to be a tall mountain rising out of the sea. The next day, as they draw nearer, they see it is a great darkness. Caspian questions whether they should enter, but Reepicheep says he hopes it will never be told in Narnia the company of noble and royal persons turned tail because they were afraid of the dark.

They are not sure how long they are in the darkness before they hear a cry for help they take on board a man Edmund thinks is the wildest he has ever seen. He yells at them to fly away as fast as they can. Reepicheep asks what the danger is. When he says this is the island where dreams come true several of the men reply favorably until the man recounts that dreams come to life on this island and suddenly they all realize there are dreams with which they do not want to live. The men run down for the oars and began to row as fast as they can. Only Reepicheep does not understand this. He asks Caspian if he is going to stand for a mutiny. Caspian tells him there are some things a man cannot face. Reepicheep replies in that case it is his good fortune not to be a man.

 Lucy considers leaving her perch on the rail of the fighting top and going down to the deck for the comfort of her brother and her friends, but she realizes each is experiencing his own terror and would be no comfort to her. She cries out to Aslan for help. Not long afterward there is a beam of light that first looks like a cross them like an airplane than a kite and then she sees an albatross. The albatross flies over and seems to guide them. No one but Lucy knows that as it circled the mast it whispered to her, "Courage to your heart," in a voice that she is sure was Aslan's. In a few moments the darkness begins to turn to gray and they find their way into the sunlight. Soon they are in the bright light and everyone is telling himself it was all just a dream. Lucy comes down to the deck and finds everyone gathered around the man they've taken on board. The man is Lord Rhoop, one of the men Caspian is seeking. He asks one thing from Caspian and that is to never be asked to tell what he saw during his years on the dark island. As they all celebrate, no one notices when the albatross disappears.

SUGGESTED ACTIVITIES CHAPTERS 11-12

1. Since the Dufflepuds face many problems that are similar to those of people with special needs, ask students to volunteer to help mentor students with special needs or give their time to help at the Special Olympics.

2. Ask students to write a short story inventing their own creatures and environment like Lewis created with the Duffers.

3. Ask students to read John 1:1-18. How is the darkness encountered by the Narnian's and the island on which dreams come true a picture of the darkness of men's souls? Have students write a compare/contrast paper explaining this concept.

VOCABULARY CHAPTERS 11-12

girdle	n	a belt, cord, sash, or the like, warn about the waist
crestfallen	adj	dejected; dispirited; discouraged
trudging	v	to walk especially wearily; tramp
monopod	n	a species with only one leg
smote	v	to affect mentally or morally with the sudden pang
inaudible	adj	incapable of being heard
parchment	n	the skin of sheep, goats, etc. prepared for use as material on which to write
sleepers	n	the timber or beam serving as a foundation or support for the rails
boatswain	n	a warrant officer on the warship, or a petty officer on a merchant vessel, in charge of rigging, anchors, cables, etc.
impeachment	n	demonstration that a witness is less worthy of belief
tiller	n	a bar or lever used for turning the rudder in steering
lurid	adj	lighted or shining with an unnatural, fiery glow
extremity	n	the extreme or terminal point, limit, or part of something
mutiny	n	rebellion against any authority, especially by sailors against officers
poltroonery	n	marked by utter cowardice
rout	n	a defeat attended with disorderly flight
albatross	n	a large web footed seabird that has the ability to remain aloft for long periods

QUESTIONS CHAPTERS 11-12

1. How does the magician feel about his subjects?

2. Where does Aslan tell Lucy and Coriakin and he is going?

3. When Lucy asks if Coriakin knew she was there all along what is his response?

4. When Lucy first sees the Duffers what does she think they are?

5. What action of the Duffers causes the magician to change them into their present form?

6. Read 1 Sam 15:22; Heb. 13:17; 1 Sam 12:15; Heb. 2:2.. How do these verses relate to the experience of the Duffers?

7. How easy is it for Lucy to persuade the Duffers that they are actually not so ugly? What does this say about people who are always willing to be led by one person?

8. What skill does Reepicheep teach the Duffers that comes in handy for them? Why do you think the Chief Duffer is hesitant at first to follow Reepicheep's suggestion?

9. What new name do the Duffers give themselves?

10. After dinner what service does the magician do for them?

11. What information is the magician not able to give them?

12. How is the ship fixed while they are on this island?

13. When they next sight what they believe to be land, what do they discover about it?

14. When Caspian is hesitant about entering the darkness how does Reepicheep encourage him to go forward?

15. When they rescue a man and take him on board, where does he say he's been stranded?

16. When the first two people put a positive spin on the concept of an island where dreams come true how does the man convince them that this is not a place where they would want to be?

17. Why is Reepicheep unable to understand the reaction of the man? Why does he see it as a mutiny?

18. When Lucy cries out to Aslan what symbol does he send to guide them out of the darkness?

19. Why is the albatross the symbol that he would send to guide them out of the darkness in the middle of the ocean?

20. When they reach the sunlight and everyone is celebrating what is the one thing no one notices? How is this similar to our experiences in life?

ANSWERS TO QUESTIONS CHAPTERS 11-12

1. He feels they're stupid but harmless, and he is looking forward to the day when he can rule them by wisdom instead of by magic.

2. He tells them he is going to Trumpkin the dwarf at Cair Paravel.

3. He tells her that he knew she would come sooner or later, but being invisible made him sleepy so he was not aware she was there at first.

4. Mushrooms

5. Instead of taking water from a nearby stream as they were asked, they instead insisted on going to a spring that was farther away, causing them to spill the water all the way back to the garden.

6. Obedience is important to God. It is important that we obey Him and that we obey those who are in authority over us. There are consequences that we must face when we are disobedient. The magician wanted the Duffers to obey him for their own good but they refused and the consequence of their disobedience was that they were changed into a different form. God also expects us to obey those who are in authority over us and if we don't obey, there will be consequences to face.

7. It is really very easy for Lucy to persuade the Duffers that they are not ugly. This is an illustration of how easy it is for people to be led by suggestion.

8. Reepicheep teaches them to use their foot as a canoe in the water. The Chief Duffer is hesitant to listen to his suggestion because he does not want to believe that anyone else can have an idea that is worthy of being followed.

9. Duffelpuds

10. The magician draws a map for them using the accounts of their travels as his reference.

11. He does not know what lies ahead of them to the east.

12. The magician magically mends the broken stern of the *Dawn Treader*.

13. Instead of being land it is actually an overwhelming darkness in front of them.

14. He tells them that he would not want to report to Narnia that the noble people aboard the ship were afraid of the dark.

15. He's been on the island where dreams come true.

16. He tells them this is the place where dreams come to life; become real.

17. Reepicheep does not understand because he doesn't have the dreams of men, particularly the nightmares of men. He sees the men's reaction as a mutiny because Caspian has not ordered them row away, and he doesn't understand the terror they are feeling.

18. Albatross

19. Albatross is a bird that can fly for long periods of time without having to land on something. Therefore, the albatross can fly above them and show them the way out of the darkness.

20. They do not notice when the albatross disappears. Often when we experience times of depression or need we call out for Jesus to help us and then when things are going well we forget to look for Him to thank Him for what He's done.

CHAPTERS 13-14

As they sail on, the sea is so smooth it is almost like they are sailing on a lake. They see constellations no one has ever seen in the skies of Narnia. Lucy thinks they probably have not been seen in any sky. The stars are so large and bright and the night so warm that they begin sleeping on the deck and talking late into the night. It is at night that they catch sight of land. This land has low-lying hills, but no mountains. There is an attractive smell that Lucy describes as purple.

Rhoop decides to stay on the ship. He has no desire to visit another island. As they first set foot on the island, it shows no sign of being inhabited. However, they see what at first appears to be large trees. Edmonds suggests they may be giants. Reepicheep responds by declaring that the only way they can tell is to get out among them. He draws his sword and marches forward. As they become closer, Lucy proclaims that she believes it is a ruin. When they are even nearer her guess is most feasible. They find an oblong space surrounded by pillars with a table covered in a crimson cloth and set with all manner of delicious food. The table is surrounded with stone chairs that have silk cushions. Eustace asks where the guests are.

Edmund quiets everyone and points to what they think at first are three beavers sitting at the table. Edmund comments that it looks like a bird's nest. Caspian replies that it is more like a haystack. Reepicheep runs along the table, examines the mass at the end of the table and proclaims he does not think they will fight; as the others discover the nondescript mounds are actually three men whose hair has grown over their faces and down their backs, over the backs of their chairs.

Caspian asks if they are dead. They are not, but are apparently asleep. Lucy observes that it must be an enchanted sleep and asks if Caspian thinks they were brought here to break the spell. He tells her they can try.

When he shakes the nearest man he seems to stir and mutters, "out oars for Narnia." He immediately returns to his slumbering state. The same result is accomplished with the other two and they realize they have found the last three Narnian lords they are seeking. The rings on their fingers confirm this.

Rhince asks why they shouldn't eat the food on the table, but Caspian replies that there is too much magic. Reepicheep concurs, adding that it is no doubt the food that has caused the three men to be in such a deep sleep.

When one of the sleepers mutters "back to the ship, back to the ship," Edmund agrees they are right and suggests they go to the ship since they can't eat the food and the place smells of magic. Reepicheep agrees with the exception that he is going to sit at the table until sunrise. When Eustace asks why, the mouse replies that it is a great adventure, and he does not want to return to Narnia having left a mystery behind through fear. Once Reepicheep decides to stay, the others will not be outdone and they also decide to stay. However, Caspian sends the crew of the ship back.

They take some time in choosing their seats, since no one wants to sit next to the three slumbering lords. They wrap themselves in their cloaks and make some attempt at conversation in the beginning. After some time they realize that they have all begun to doze and suddenly they are wide-awake. They realize the stars are in a different position from the last time they noticed them.

They see a doorway opening in a hillside and a figure carrying a light emerging from the doorway. They can make out that the figure is a tall girl dressed in a single long garment of blue. She has long blonde hair and she's very beautiful. She carries a tall candle in a silver candlestick which she sets upon the table.

Lucy notices something she has not noticed before, which is a knife of stone that is sharp and cruel looking lying on the table. Reepicheep moves first and then the others, rising to their feet in respect for her as a great lady.

She asks why they have not eaten any of the food. Caspian explains that they have feared the food was enchanted and caused the men to be in a deep sleep. She explains the men have never tasted the food. She tells them that the men came seven years ago and when they came to this table they began to argue with each other. As they quarreled one of them caught up the Knife of Stone which lies on the table and would have fought with the others. The girl explains it is not a thing that is right for him to touch. As soon as his fingers closed on the hilt a deep sleep fell on all three.

Eustace asks what the Knife of Stone is. The girl asks if they know of it. Lucy replies that she has seen something like it before. The White Witch used it to kill Aslan on the Stone Table long ago. The girl replies that it is the same and it must be kept in honor while the world lasts.

Edmund has been looking more and more uncomfortable. He asks the girl how they can know she's a friend. She says she doesn't know. They can believe her or not. Reepicheep asks Caspian to fill his cup with wine and he will drink to the lady. Caspian obeys and Reepicheep pledges his honor to the lady. Soon they all are eating and fill themselves with a fine breakfast.

Lucy asks why it is called Aslan's Table. The girl replies it is set here at his bidding for those who come so far. Eustace asks how the food keeps. The girl explains the food is eaten and renewed every day. Caspian asks what they should do about the sleepers. The girl tells them that her father will tell them how the enchantment can be taken off. They look and see the door has opened in the hillside and another figure as tall and straight is the girl is coming. This figure does not carry a light but light seems to come from it. Lucy sees he is an old man. His silver beard comes down to his bare feet and his silver hair hangs to his heels behind.

His robe appears to be made from the fleece of a silver sheep.

The old man comes and stands without speaking close to the travelers, but on the other side of his daughter. They hold hands and face the East and begin to sing. Afterwards Lucy says it was a high, almost shrill song, but very beautiful. As they sing the East begins to turn red. At last, unclouded, the sun begins to come out of the sea and its rays shoot down the length of the table on the gold and silver and on the stone knife. Immediately hundreds and thousands of birds appear and light everywhere on the grass, on the pavement, on the table, and cover everything. One of the birds takes something in its beak that looks like a little fruit but seems like live coal and places it in the old man's mouth. Soon the birds completely clean everything that's on the table.

When the birds are gone the old man turns to the travelers. Caspian asks him how they can undo the enchantment which holds the Narnian lords. He replies they must sail to the world's end and return having left at least one of their company there. Reepicheep inquires what will happen to that one. The old man says he must go into the utter East and never return into the world. Reepicheep says that is his heart's desire.

Caspian asks how far they are from the world's end. The old man tells them he saw it long ago but he was flying above. Eustace asks how he was flying in the air. He replies he is Ramandu. He is a star that ceased being a star. He explains that when he set for the last time he was carried to this island. Eustace says that in his world a star is a huge ball of flaming gas..Ramandu replies that even in his world that's not what a star is, that only what it is made of.

Ramandu tells the children they have met a star before, because Coriakin was also a star. Lucy asks if he was also a retired star. Ramandu explains that Coriakin has been sent where he is as punishment. Caspian asks what he did. Ramandu responds that it is not for Caspian to know. Ramandu asks if Caspian is resolved to sail East or if he's going to return to the West. Caspian is concerned about the crew of the *Dawn Treader*. Reepicheep agrees the men are weary. Caspian brings up Lord Rhoop, who is a broken man. Ramandu instructs Caspian to bring the man onto the island and he will give him rest which will be healing.

As they eat that evening, Caspian gives the men the option of sailing on with him or waiting on the island until he returns. Only one man chooses to stay. Before they leave Caspian tells Ramandu's daughter he hopes to speak to her again when he has broken all the enchantments. She smiles at him.

SUGGESTED ACTIVITIES CHAPTERS 13-14

1. Ask students to collect canned goods for a local food pantry or participate in a ministry that helps to feed the homeless.

2. Ask students to write a journal entry from the perspective of one of the crew members who has to make the decision whether to continue with Caspian or stay on the island.

3. Have students illustrate Ramandu, his daughter, or the three sleeping lords.

<u>VOCABULARY CHAPTERS 13-14</u>

luminous	adj	radiating or reflecting light; shining; bright
habitation	n	a place of residence; dwelling; abode
botany	n	the science of plants; the branch of biology that deals with plant life
flagons	n	a large bottle for wine, liquors, etc.
turf	n	a layer of matted earth formed by grass and plant roots
perilous	adj	involving or full of grave risk or peril; hazardous; dangerous
sauntered	v	to walk with a leisurely gait; stroll
distinctly	adv	without doubt; unmistakably
hilt	n	the handle of a sword or dagger
grave	adj	serious or solemn; sober
decrepit	adj	weakened by old age; feeble; infirm
resolved	adj	firm in purpose or intent; determined
stint	n	a period of time spent doing something
oblivion	n	the state of forgetting or of being oblivious
quay	n	a landing place constructed along the edge of a body of water; wharf
bequeath	v	to dispose of personal property by last will

QUESTIONS CHAPTERS 13-14

1. What changes take place as the voyage continues?

2. Lucy describes smell of the island as a purple kind of smell. What do you think of purple kind of smell would smell like?

3. What do they find that is the first indication that the island is inhabited?

4. How do they know for sure they have found the three Narnian lords?

5. What leads them to the conclusion that the food is the source of the enchantment on the **men**?

6. Why do they decide to spend the night sitting around the table?

7. When they realize they've been dozing and wake up what do they see?

8. Describe the girl that comes to them.

9. What does Lucy notice that she has not noticed before?

10. What name does the girl give to the table?

11. What explanation does she give as to why the Narnian lords have been put into the deep sleep?

12. What does Lucy recall about the Knife of Stone?

13. Who is the first to accept the girl's words as true and give her respect as a lady?

14. How is the table cleaned?

15. Who is the girl's father? What is his story? Who else have they met that was a star?

16. What does Ramandu tell them must be done in order to break the enchantment on the three nobles?

17. What difficulty does Caspian bring up and discuss with Reepicheep? How is it settled?

18. What solution is offered for Lord Rhoop?

19. What question does the master Bowman bring up? What is the answer?

20. How many of the crew decide to stay on the island while Caspian continues to the world's end?

ANSWERS TO QUESTIONS CHAPTERS 13-14

1. The wind doesn't fail but it becomes gentler every day and the waves are like little ripples so that the ship is gliding on hour after hour as if they're sailing on a lake. Every night they see constellations that are unlike any they have seen in Narnia; maybe unlike any that anyone has seen anywhere. The nights are also very warm and they are able to sleep on the deck.

2. Answers will vary.

3. They find an oblong area enclosed by pillars in which there is a table set with all kinds of delicacies.

4. First they hear the man speaking of returning to Narnia in their sleep. Their identification is confirmed when they see the rings on the men's fingers.

5. Reepicheep is the first to conclude that the food is the source of the enchantment. Caspian agrees with them and tells the others not to touch the food.

6. Reepicheep makes the decision to sit at the table throughout the night because he does not want to miss out on any adventure due to fear. The others do not want to be outdone by the mouse and decide to join him.

7. They see a door opening in the hillside and the female figure coming to the door.

8. The girl is very tall with long blonde hair. She's wearing a long dress of clear blue that is sleeveless. She is carrying a tall candle in a silver candlestick.

9. There is a knife on the table that is made of stone, sharp as steel and very cruel looking. It is an ancient looking thing.

10. Aslan's Table

11. The three lords had landed on the island seven years before. They were quarreling and one of them picked up the Stone Knife and would have used it. The girl explains that it was not his place to touch it. The spell was then put on the three men that cause them to sleep.

12. It is the knife that belonged to the White Witch and was used to kill Aslan on the Stone Table.

13. Reepicheep

14. Birds arrive and flock all over the area, completely cleaning the table.

15. The girl's father is named Ramandu. He explains that he is a star in resting. The other star they have met is Coriakin the magician.

16. They must sail to the end of the world and leave at least one of their members behind, then return.

17. Many of the men are weary and Caspian is afraid they will be unwilling to continue for the rest of the voyage. They are given the option of staying on the island and waiting while those who desire to continue the adventure continue.

18. Ramandu tells them to bring Lord Rhoop onto the island and he will put in enchantment on him that will help them to rest so that he can have healing.

19. How will they be able to return home since the winds have always been in a westerly direction carrying them away from Narnia and it will be impossible for them to roll all the way back to Narnia? Drinian explains that the winds change after the new year and they will have plenty of land to take them home at that time. One of the sailors suggests that they stay on the island during January and February and start the voyage home in March.

20. One

CHAPTERS 15-16

After leaving Ramandu's country it seems that everything changes. No one wants to sleep or eat much. When the sun comes up it looks to Lucy three times its usual size. Every morning they see the huge white birds heading to Ramandu's island, singing their song in human voices but in a language no one recognizes.

The water is so clear Lucy can observe the shadow of the ship on the sea floor below. She also recognizes what appears to be a road. The road runs through an area of vegetation and then re-emerges. She sees the road intersect with another road and then realizes it is becoming closer to the surface. The road begins to go in zigzags, obviously climbing up a steep hill. As the road reaches the top of the hill, Lucy sees little specks moving to and fro and realizes they must be some kind of creatures.

At the top of the hill she spies a huge castle and wonders why it is built on a high mountain. Later when she and Edmund and Eustace are in England they talk it over and decide that a mountain must be the best place to build a castle under the sea. The valleys would be the places where the sea serpents and squids and other creatures will live.

They pass the city and Lucy nearly squeals with delight when she sees people riding seahorses out on the plain. The sea people are using fish to hunt in the same way that Lucy and Edmund used to use Falcons when they were kings and queens in Narnia long ago. The Sea People have ivory skin and dark purple hair. They all wear some kind of Coronet and have chains of pearls. When they see the ship passing above them, they have looks of astonishment on their faces.

Drinian and Edmund ask what she's looking at. When she shows them, Drinian informs her that she should not allow the other

sailors to know about the Sea People. They will fall in love with the sea women or fall in love with the undersea country itself and jump overboard. Lucy mentions Sea People who sang at their coronation at Cair Paravel. Edmund replies they must have been a different kind, because they could live in the air as well as in the sea.

They are interrupted by two sounds, a plop and the sound of "Man overboard." It isn't actually a man that has gone overboard but a mouse – it is Reepicheep. The *Dawn Treader* is turned around and when they find Reepicheep he is quite excited. He keeps chattering but his mouth keeps filling up with water. Drinian is afraid he will blurt out the information about the Sea People and rushes to his side as soon as the mouse is pulled on board. He leans over and tells Reepicheep not to say a word. However, what Reepicheep is excited about is that the water is no longer saltwater but is sweet. He repeats the words of the old prophecy: "where the waves grow sweet, doubt not, Reepicheep, there is the utter East."

A bucket of water is brought on board and each of them drink some of it. They find it to be not only sweet, but so strong that they feel they do not need to eat anything. The water also makes it so that they are able to look into the sun. Drinian notices that there is no wind and yet they continue to move as fast as if there is a gale behind them. Caspian says they must be caught in some kind of strong current. Edmund replies that won't be so nice if the world really has an edge and they're getting near it. Reepicheep finds this to be exciting, clapping his hands and exclaiming that this is how he has always imagined it; the waters of all the oceans endlessly pouring over the edge. When he describes how the ship will tip up and go over the edge and then go down, down, over the edge Drinian asks what he thinks will be waiting for them at the bottom. Reepicheep replies Aslan's country perhaps or perhaps there isn't any bottom. Eustace chimes in to say that the world is round. Edmund says our world is but is this? Caspian is fascinated with the idea of a round world. He doesn't understand why the other children can get into his world but he cannot get into theirs. Edmund tells him there's nothing that exciting about a round world when you're there.

Only Reepicheep, Drinian, and the two Pevensies saw the Sea People before, and only Lucy sees anything more of them. The following day Lucy sees a little Sea Girl about her age with a crook in her hand tending to a large shoal of fish. She realizes the girl is a shepherdess. They see each other and they both like each other.

The ship continues for many days and every day the light becomes more brilliant. No one eats or sleeps because they don't want to, but the water from the sea helps them become stronger. Sailors who were older men when they started the voyage become younger every day. Everyone is filled with joy and excitement.

One day Caspian asks Drinian what he sees ahead. All they can see his whiteness, and Drinian replies he would say it was ice if they were in higher latitudes. Drinian tells them they need to take out the oars so they won't crash into it head on. They are not able to make out what the whiteness is and they finally decide to lower a boat and send a party out to investigate. Soon the voices come back saying they are lilies. Caspian asks for clarification and Rynelf repeats again that they are lilies just like would be in the pool and garden at home. Drinian asks what the depth of the water is, and Rynelf replies three and a half fathoms. Eustace says they can't be real lilies. And though they probably were not they were very much like them the decision is made to turn the *Dawn Treader* back into the current and glide eastward through the Lily Lake or the Silver Sea (it was named the Silver Sea on Caspian's map).

Continuing through the whiteness makes the daylight last longer. If their eyes had not been so strong the early morning sun would be unbearable to them. Day after day they continue through the miles and miles of flowers. There arises a smell from the flowers which Lucy and Caspian say to one another that," I feel that I can't stand much more of this yet I don't want to stop."

There comes a point when the ship can go no further because the water is too shallow. Caspian orders them to lower the boat and calls the men. He tells the men that they have fulfilled the quest on which they have embarked: the seven lords are all accounted for and since Reepicheep has sworn never to return, they can return to Ramandu's Land and the spell will have been lifted on the three lords there. He is entrusting the ship to them and abdicating his position as King. He is planning to go with Reepicheep.

Edmund, Reepicheep, and Drinian urge Caspian not to do what he's planning to do. When they tell him he can't, he gives them a look that is similar to his uncle Miraz. He tells them he thinks they are all his subjects not his schoolmasters. Edmund tells him he is not and he says that Caspian cannot do this. Caspian asks what he means. Reepicheep chimes in and says that they mean he shall not. He would break faith with all of his subjects and especially with Trumpkin if he does not return. Lucy adds that he has almost promised Ramandu's daughter he will return. When Reepicheep reminds Caspian of his promise to allow the mouse to stay behind, Caspian becomes enraged and goes to his cabin, slamming the door behind him.

Caspian emerges later to say that Aslan has visited him and told him that Reepicheep, Edmund, Lucy, and Eustace would have to go and Caspian must return by himself. Lucy tells him he will feel better when he gets back to Ramandu's Land.

About 2 o'clock the boat is lowered and the *Dawn Treader* turns and moves westward while those in the boat continue toward the east. All that night and the next day they continue going east and then when the sun comes up the next day they see a wall that looks like a huge wave. As they look they see something that is behind the wave and behind the sun. They see a range of mountains so high that they either never see the top or they forget that they can see the top of it. Suddenly the boat is aground because the water is too shallow for even it. Reepicheep tells them that this is where he goes it alone. They help him lower his little coracle. He takes off his sword and flings it far away across the lilied sea. It lands in a position where it is standing upright with the hilt above the surface. When he tells them goodbye, Lucy does what she's always wanted to do; takes him in her arms and caresses him. Reepicheep takes his paddle, catches the current and vanishes over the very top of the wave. No one's ever seen Reepicheep again.

The children get out of the boat and wade southward. They hold hands as they walk. In front of them is a huge plain where the grass seems to meet with the sky, and at the foot of the sky there is something white on the green grass. As they come near to it they see it's a lamb. The lamb invites them to breakfast. As they eat, Lucy asks if this is the way to Aslan's country. The lamb replies that for them the door to Aslan's country is from their own world. When Edmund asks if there's a way into Aslan's country from their world also the lamb turns into Aslan himself. He tells them that there is a way into his country from all worlds. Lucy asks if he'll tell them how to get into his country from their world. Aslan replies he will be telling them all the time. He tells them he's the great bridge builder and he will open the door in the sky and send them to their own land.

Lucy wants to know when they can come back to Narnia again, but Aslan tells them that she and Edmund are too old and will never return. Lucy sobs, telling Aslan it's not Narnia, but Aslan she wants to come to see. Aslan tells her she will meet him in her own world too. Lucy asks if Eustace will come back here. Aslan tells her she doesn't really need to know that. There's an opening in the blue wall and the children find themselves back in the bedroom in an Alberta's home in Cambridge.

Caspian's men arrive safely back at Ramandu's Island. The three lords wake from their sleep. Caspian marries Ramandu's daughter and they all reach Narnia in the end. Ramandu's daughter becomes a great Queen and mother and grandmother of great kings.

SUGGESTED ACTIVITIES CHAPTERS 15-16

1. Caspian comes close to abdicating his throne in these chapters. Ask students to do research into Richard the Lionhearted, who did not abdicate, but by going on a crusade, much like Caspian's quest, lost his life and his kingdom. Other suggestions would be King Edward VIII of England, Mary Queen of Scots, Lucius Cornelius Sulla the Dictator in 79 BC, EmperorDiocletian in AD 305, and Emperor Romulus Augustulus in AD 476.

2. Ask students to illustrate one of the scenes from these chapters.

3. The climax of the book occurs when Caspian faces the conflict between his selfish desire to go on with Reepicheep and his responsibility to fulfill his duties as King of Narnia. Ask students to identify the climax and the conflict that Caspian is facing. Ask them why this is such a difficult situation to face.

VOCABULARY CHAPTERS 15-16

expanse	n	an uninterrupted space or area; a wide extent of anything
submarine	adj	living under the surface of the sea
shafts	n	a ray or beam
pinnacles	n	a relatively small, upright structure, commonly terminating in a gable, a pyramid, or a cone
minarets	n	a lofty, often slender, tower or turret attached to a mosque
kraken	n	a legendary sea monster causing large whirlpools off the coast of Norway
quests	n	an adventurous expedition undertaken by a knight to secure or achieve something
Coronet	n	a small crown
keel hauled	v	to rebuke severely
marooned	v	to put ashore and abandon on a desolate island by way of punishment
consultation	n	a meeting for deliberation, discussion, or decision
abdicating	v	to renounce or relinquish a throne, especially in a formal manner
dismay	n	sudden or complete loss of courage; utter disheartenment
presume	v	to act or proceed with unwarrantable or impertinent boldness
irresolute	adj	doubtful; infirm of purpose; vacillating
grievous	adj	causing great pain or suffering
rending	v	to tear apart, split, or divide

QUESTIONS CHAPTERS 15-16

1. After leaving Ramandu's land how, do things change?

2. As Lucy notices how clear the water is, what she see on the bottom?

3. When Lucy first sees the city under the sea where is it built? What does she decide is the reason for this?

4. When Lucy sees the Sea People what are they doing?

5. What happens that causes Drinian to fear that the sailors will want to jump in and follow the sea people?

6. Reepicheep is not fascinated by the Sea People, but by what attribute of the water?

7. When they begin to drink the water what does it do for them?

8. Read John 4:13 – 14. How does the water described in these verses compare to the water described in the chapters you have just read?

9. Why is Reepicheep so excited?

10. What is Reepicheep's idea of going over the edge of the world?

11. When Eustace says that their world is round what does Caspian bring up?

12. When Caspian is fascinated by the idea of around the world what does Edmund tell him? What does this say about human nature?

13. When Caspian tells the men he's going to abdicate and go with Reepicheep to see the world's end why do they tell him that he can't do this? What does this say about responsibility?

14. Who finally convinces Caspian that he must fulfill his responsibility to Narnia?

15. What does Aslan have to say to Lucy and Edmund that they find hard to hear?

16. When Lucy tells Aslan it's not Narnia but meeting him that is causing her grief what is his reply?

17. Why does Aslan tell them that in their world he's known by another name? What is the name?

18. When Lucy asks if Eustace is going to come back how does Aslan respond?

19. What becomes of Caspian and his men?

20. Characters can be dynamic or static. Dynamic characters change during the course of the novel. Static characters stay the same. Which kind is Eustace? Why?

ANSWERS TO QUESTIONS CHAPTERS 15-16

1. They need less sleep, they find they do not want to go to bed nor want to eat much. When the sun comes up it looks twice if not three times as usual size. Every morning they see the huge white birds streaming overhead on their way to Aslan's table and afterwards they fly back vanishing into the East.

2. She sees the shadow of the *Dawn Treader* on the floor of the sea underneath them.

3. The city is built on the top of a mountain. She decides later that there's more protection on top of the mountain because the dangerous things like sea monsters and squids and the Kraken live in the valleys under the sea.

4. They are hunting, using fish just as she and Edmund used Falcons when they were kings and queens in Narnia long ago.

5. Reepicheep jumps overboard.

6. The water is no longer saltwater but is sweet.

7. It causes them to feel strong, it helps them to look into the sun without hurting their eyes, and it allows them to go without eating.

8. Although the water described in John's spiritual water it provides for us in supernatural ways. The verses say that if we drink from his water we will not thirst again. The water that the voyagers on the *Dawn Treader* experienced is also a form of supernatural water because it provides not only for the thirst of those on board but also gives them strength and keeps them from being hungry.

9. The sweet water is a fulfillment of the prophecy that has led him on this quest to begin with.

10. He describes the world as a great roundtable and the waters of all the oceans pouring over the edge. He believes the ship will tip up stand on her head and then go over the edge rushing down, down, over the edge.

11. Caspian wonders why the other children can get into his world but he can't get into theirs.

12. Edmund tells him there's nothing particularly exciting about living in a round world when you're there. This is an example of the principal that "the grass is always greener on the other side." Each boy thinks the other one's world is more exciting than his own, **and this** is often true of anything in human nature.

13. He will be letting down the citizens of Narnia and especially Trumpkin if he does not return. He has responsibilities as the king and cannot just go off and have adventures and leave his responsibilities behind. This teaches us that those in leadership have a great responsibility to those they lead.

14. Aslan

15. They will not return to Narnia because they have become too old.

16. She will know him in her world but by a different name.

17. In our world he is known as the Lord Jesus Christ.

18. He asks if she really needs to know.

19. They returned to Ramandu's Land, where Caspian marries Ramandu's daughter. They then returned to Narnia.

20. Eustace is a dynamic character, because he changes radically from the beginning of the book to the end. In the beginning, he whines and complains about everything and is very difficult to get along with. By the end of the book he has learned to get along with others and has developed a more pleasing personality.

VOYAGE OF THE DAWN TREADER
VOCABULARY TEST CHAPTERS 1-2

I.   **Multiple Choice: Circle the letter of the correct number:**

1. When Eustace uses "Narnia" and "balmier" in a poem, he explains to Edmund he is using **assonance**, which is:
    a.   Showing bad manners; impolite; rude
    b.   A very short time; an instant
    c.   Unusual or strange; odd
    d.   The use of the same vowel sound with different consonants

2. Just as the children got their balance, a "great blue **roller** surged up round them:"
    a.   Of the human body; bodily; physical
    b.   A long heavy wave of the sea, advancing toward the shore
    c.   Of less than normal size and strength; weak
    d.   A small sword, having a narrow blade and used for thrusting

3. Lucy knew the lamps were the work of dwarves by their **exquisite** delicacy:
    a.   bending readily without breaking or becoming deformed
    b.   unusual or strange; odd; different
    c.   covered or highlighted with gold or something of a golden color
    d.   extraordinarily fine or admirable

4. Edmund tells Caspian it has been a year by their time since his **coronation**:
    a.   the quality of being new and fresh and interesting
    b.   a strenuous effort; attempt
    c.   the act or ceremony of crowning a monarch
    d.   one who seizes power without proper authority

5. Caspian explains that he has sworn an oath that once piece was established in Narnia he would sail east for a year and a day to find his father's friends or learn of their deaths and **avenge** them if he could:
    a.   terrifying; horrible
    b.   take revenge for or on behalf of
    c.   to bring (a charge or accusation) against someone
    d.   to spread out, expand, or extend

6. Reepicheep explains to them that they are now more than 400 **leagues** from Narnia:
    a.   a distance of about 3 miles
    b.   of less than normal size and strength, week
    c.   a very short time; an instant
    d.   a small sword, having a narrow blade and used for thrusting

7. When they started to tour the ship, they went up on the **forecastle** and saw the lookout man:
    a.   a superstructure at the stern of a vessel
    b.   a merchant vessel having various rigs
    c.   the kitchen of a ship, boat, or aircraft
    d.   the part of a vessel at the bow where the crew is quartered and stores, machines, etc. may be stowed

8. Caspian's uncle Miraz was a **usurper**:
   a. a wretched coward; craven
   b. one who seizes power without proper authority
   c. a person who is opposed to war or violence of any kind
   d. a person who abstains totally from intoxicating drink

9. Eustace writes in his journal that the first 24 hours have been **ghastly**:
   a. moody, surly, morose, churlish
   b. marked by lack of taste, culture, delicacy, manners, etc.
   c. terrifying; horrible
   d. showing bad manners; impolite; rude

10. When Reepicheep hits Eustace with the side of his rapier Eustace finds the sensation to be a complete **novelty**:
   a. a strenuous effort; attempt
   b. the quality of being new and fresh and interesting
   c. the final settlement of a matter
   d. a very short time; an instant

II.   Matching: Place the letter of the correct answer in the blank:

1._____teetotalers   A. to incline to one side; careen

2._____puny   B. unusual or strange; odd

3._____prow   C. a strenuous effort; attempt

4._____gilded   D. of less than normal size and strength; weak

5._____listing   E. showing bad manners; impolite; rude

6._____briny   F. a person who abstains totally from intoxicating drink

7._____endeavours   G. the forepart of a ship or boat

8._____vulgar   H. salty

9._____singularly   I. covered or highlighted with gold or a golden color

10._____discourteous   J. marked by a lack of taste, culture, delicacy, manners, etc.

III. Matching: Place the letter of the correct answer in the blank:

1. _____galley   A. to spread out, expand, or extend

2. _____victual   B. the final settlement of a matter

3. _____poop   C. a person who is opposed to war or violence of any kind

4. _____lodge   D. food supplies; provisions

5. _____disposition   E. an officer on a warship

6. _____sulkily   F. the kitchen of a ship, boat or aircraft

7. _____boatswain   G. a wretched coward; craven

8. _____splayed   H. to bring a charge or accusation against someone

9. _____poltroon   I. moody, surly, morose, churlish

10. _____pacifist   J. a superstructure at the stern of a vessel

IV. True/False: Write T or F in the blank:

1. _____ Corporal is a kind of sailing ship used during the Middle Ages.

2. _____ If you were with Caspian, you might sail on a rapier.

3. _____When Lucy and Edmund ruled Narnia, they had a fleet of ships which included cogs, dromonds, carracks and galleons.

4. _____Reepicheep's sword was supple, which means it would break easily.

5. _____A trice is an instant.

VOYAGE OF THE DAWN TREADER
VOCABULARY TEST CHAPTERS 1-2
ANSWER KEY

I. **Multiple Choice:**
1. d
2. b
3. d
4. c
5. b
6. a
7. d
8. b
9. c
10. b

II. **Matching:**
1. F
2. D
3. G
4. I
5. A
6. H
7. C
8. J
9. B
10. E

III. **Matching:**
1. F
2. D
3. J
4. H
5. B
6. I
7. E
8. A
9. G
10. C

IV. **True/False:**
1. F
2. F
3. T
4. F
5. T

VOYAGE OF THE DAWN TREADER
VOCABULARY TEST CHAPTERS 3-4

I. Fill in the Blank: Use the Word Bank below to fill in the blanks:

1. As they prepare to leave the Lone Islands, with the *Dawn Treader* fully supplied, Edmund noticed with disappointment this only gave them a _____ eastward sailing.

2. Caspian told the guards in the Governor's court that he wanted to see them looking like men at arms and not _____.

3. Caspian was sorry for the others _____ in the hold of Pug's ship.

4. Lord Bern told Pug he did not want to listen to the _____ of his filthy trade.

5. Reepicheep _____ to ride on Lucy's shoulder.

6. Edmund says that Felimath was_____ in their day and probably is still the same.

7. Lucy kicked off her shoes while swimming, but that is no hardship if one is going to walk on downy_____.

8. Caspian asked Gumpas why he had permitted this_____ and unnatural traffic in slaves to grow up here.

9. The Duke asks whether they will leave without a_____ or with one.

10. Gumpas had seen a ship signaling, as he supposed, to its_____.

Word Bank:

Consented	flogging	languishing	fortnight	consorts
Uninhabited	abominable	vagabonds	rigamarole	turf

II. Matching: Place the letter of the correct answer in the blank

1._____remote   A. rottenness; anything vile

2._____writhing   B. a territory held in fee

3._____infuriated   C. a back door or gate

4._____suffocated   D. to make furious; enrage

5._____bedraggled   E. out-of-the-way; secluded

6._____carrion   F. a landing pier; dock

7._____disbursed   G. to smother

8._____fief   H. to twist the body about, or squirm, as in pain

9._____jetty   I. limp and soiled, as with rain or dirt

10._____postern   J. to pay out money, especially for expenses; expend

III. Matching: Place the letter of the correct answer in the blank:

1._____gauntleted   A. the lower classes; the common people

2._____dandified   B. a search or pursuit to find or obtain something

3._____dossiers   C. wearing a mediaeval protective glove

4._____rabble   D. irritating, exasperating, or bitterly humiliating

5._____galling   E. a collection or file of documents with detailed
                                 Information about a person or topic

6._____quest   F. affecting extreme elegance in dress and manner

<u>VOYAGE OF THE DAWN TREADER</u>
<u>VOCABULARY TEST CHAPTERS 3-4</u>
<u>ANSWER KEY</u>

I. **Fill in the Blank**:
1. Fortnight
2. Vagabonds
3. Languishing
4. Rigamarole
5. Consented
6. Uninhabited
7. Turf
8. Abominable
9. Flogging
10. Consorts

II. **Matching:**
1. E
2. H
3. D
4. G
5. I
6. A
7. J
8. B
9. F
10. C

III. **Matching:**

1. C
2. F
3. E
4. A
5. D
6. B

VOYAGE OF THE DAWN TREADER
VOCABULARY TEST CHAPTERS 5-6

I.   Multiple Choice: Circle the letter of the correct choice:

1. Reepicheep's mind was full of **forlorn** hopes, death or glory charges, and last stands:
    a.   bad, evil, base, or wicked
    b.   burdensome, unjustly harsh, or tyrannical
    c.   lonely and sad: forsaken
    d.   characterized by great caution, secrecy, etc.; furtive

2. A **cataract** of water poured over the deck:
    a.   a long narrow arm of the sea bordered by steep cliffs
    b.   a cliff with a vertical, nearly vertical, or overhanging face
    c.   to board a ship, aircraft, or other vehicle, as for a journey
    d.   a descent of water over a steep surface

3. Eustace wrote in his journal that it was "pleasant to be **embarked** on a dangerous voyage with people who can't even count right:"
    a.   to board a ship, aircraft, or other vehicle, is for a journey
    b.   to turn, swing, twist
    c.   to make a false show of something; pretend
    d.   to cause a vessel to incline to one side

4. Eustace says that it would be hard enough if one was with decent people instead of **fiends** in human form:
    a.   a person who is smugly and self -righteously narrowminded
    b.   a diabolically cruel or wicked person
    c.   causing dismay or horror
    d.   a contemptible, worthless person

5. The scene would have been pretty in a picture but was rather **oppressive** in real life:
    a.   causing dismay or horror
    b.   lonely and sad or second
    c.   bending readily; plant; limber; supple; flexible
    d.   burdensome, unjustly harsh, or tyrannical

6. The valley was so narrow and deep and the **precipices** which surrounded it so share that it was like a huge pit or trench:
    a.   a supply or accumulation that is hidden or carefully guarded
    b.   a cliff with a vertical, nearly vertical, or overhanging face
    c.   a long, narrow arm of the sea bordered by steep cliffs
    d.   a descent of water over a steep surface

7. When Eustace could hold his breath no longer he let it out **stealthily;** instantly two jets of smoke appeared again:
    a.   characterized by great caution, secrecy, etc.; furtive
    b.   causing anxiety or uneasiness; disturbing
    c.   highly offensive: repugnant; disgusting
    d.   bad, evil, base, or wicked

8. Eustace had turned into a dragon by sleeping on a dragon's **hoard** with greedy, dragon-ish thoughts in his heart:
   a. a contemptible, worthless person
   b. a thick soled, laced boot or half boot
   c. a person who is smugly and self- righteously narrowminded
   d. a supply or accumulation that is hidden or carefully guarded

9. When Caspian came **back** from looking for Eustace, the news was **disquieting**:
   a. having a superior manner; condescending
   b. causing anxiety or uneasiness; disturbing
   c. highly offensive; repugnant; disgusting
   d. causing dismay or horror

10. Lucy was noticing these things and wondering about the **sinister** change that had come over the very noise of the wind:
    a. lonely and sad to me: forsaken
    b. bending readily; pliant; limber; supple; flexible
    c. bad, evil, base, or wicked
    d. highly offensive; repugnant; disgusting

II. Matching: Place the letter of the correct answer in the blank:

1._____prow	A. causing dismay or horror
2._____buskins	B. to cover a hatch so as to make watertight
3._____jerkins	C. having a superior manner; condescending
4._____battened	D. to cause a vessel to incline to one side
5._____reef	E. a thick soled, laced boot or half boot
6._____listing	F. a person who is smugly, self- righteously narrowminded
7._____appalling	G. the forepart of a ship or boat; bow
8._____wireless	H. to shorten a sale by tying in one or more reefs
9._____prig	I. a close fitted jacket or coat, usually sleeveless
10._____patronizing	J. chiefly British, radio

III. Matching: Place the letter of the correct answer in the blank:

1. _____ odious   A. a contemptible, worthless person

2. _____ fjiord   B. to make a false show of something; pretend

3. _____ blighter   C. bending readily; pliant; limber; supple; flexible

4. _____ slewed   D. a long narrow arm of the sea bordered by steep cliffs

5. _____ lithe   E. to turn, swing, twist

6. _____ shamming   F. highly offensive; repugnant; disgusting

VOYAGE OF THE DAWN TREADER
VOCABULARY TEST CHAPTERS 5-6
ANSWER KEY

I. **Multiple Choice:**
1. c
2. d
3. a
4. b
5. d
6. b
7. a
8. d
9. b
10. c

II. **Matching:**
1. G
2. E
3. I
4. B
5. H
6. D
7. A
8. J
9. F
10. C

III. **Matching:**
1. F
2. D
3. A
4. E
5. C
6. B

VOYAGE OF THE DAWN TREADER
VOCABULARY TEST CHAPTERS 7-10

I. **Multiple Choice: Circle the letter of the correct answer:**

1. Reepicheep said that it was folly to think of avoiding an invisible enemy by any amount of creeping and **skulking:**
   a. to fall back into a former state
   b. to move in a stealthy manner; slink
   c. to count, compute, or calculate
   d. to hold an informal conference with an enemy under a truce

2. Lucy assures them that the invisible voices are not **treacherous:**
   a. eager; interested; enthusiastic
   b. not softened or lessened
   c. absolutely trustworthy or sure
   d. characterized by faithlessness or readiness to betray trust; traitorous

3. Suddenly an appalling head reared itself out of the sea. It was all greens and **vermilions** with purple blotches:
   a. filth, dirt, or slime
   b. a facial expression, often ugly or contorted
   c. a brilliant red
   d. of feeling or condition of hostility; hatred; ill will

4. Although Eustace was a new boy he had **relapses:**
   a. an act of falling back into a former state or practice
   b. unrestrained or violent anger, rage, passion, or the like
   c. the act of offering or suggesting something for acceptance
   d. of feeling or condition of hostility; hatred; ill will

5. Lucy heard soft heavy footfalls coming along the <u>corridor</u> behind her:
   a. a small roundish boat made of skins stretched on a wicker frame
   b. a hammer like tool with a head commonly of wood
   c. a gallery or passage connecting parts of the building; hallway
   d. descriptive of any hard stone that splits and is suitable for paving

6. Lucy read an **infallible** spell to make beautiful her that other of it beyond the lot of mortals:
   a. not softened or lessened
   b. absolutely trustworthy or sure
   c. eager; interested; enthusiastic
   d. easily seen or noticed; readily visible

7. Everyone praised the **valor** of Eustace and of Reepicheep:
   a. an abrupt, exclamatory utterance
   b. the state or quality of being foolish
   c. of or pertaining to human beings as subject to death; human
   d. boldness or determination when facing danger

8. Eustace realized that from the first day he came on board he had been an **<u>unmitigated</u>** nuisance:
   a. unqualified or absolute
   b. easily seen or noticed; readily visible
   c. Eager; interested; enthusiastic
   d. absolutely trustworthy or sure

9. Lucy saw a spell that would make her beautiful beyond the lot of **<u>mortals:</u>**
   a. a hammer like tool with ahead commonly of wood
   b. the state or quality of being foolish
   c. of or pertaining to human beings as subject to death; human
   d. the act of offering or suggesting something for acceptance

10. On the island they found a small **<u>coracle</u>** on The Sands:
    a. an informal name for tobacco
    b. a small roundish boat made of skins stretched on a wicker frame
    c. food supplies; provisions
    d. a gallery or passage connecting parts of the building; hallway

11. Caspian and the others went back to the path where the trees might possibly make them less **<u>conspicuous</u>**:
    a. characterized by faithlessness or readiness to betray trust; traitorous
    b. causing great dread, fear, or terror
    c. eager; interested; enthusiastic
    d. easily seen or noticed; readily visible

12. Eustace tells Edmund he is very **<u>inquisitive</u>** about these people:
    a. given to inquiry, research, or asking questions, eager for knowledge
    b. eager; interested; enthusiastic
    c. absolutely trustworthy or sure
    d. makes things together in a confused or disordered way

13. Edmund says that Lucy is not too **<u>keen</u>** on insects:
    a. unqualified or absolute
    b. easily seen or noticed; readily visible
    c. eager; interested; enthusiastic
    d. given to inquiry, research, or asking questions, eager for knowledge

14. Lucy was almost certain that a wicked little bearded face popped out of the wall and made a **<u>grimace</u>** at her:
    a. an abrupt, exclamatory utterance
    b. a facial expression, often ugly or contorted, that indicates disapproval, pain, etc.
    c. unrestrained or violent anger, rage, passion, or the like
    d. the state or quality of being foolish

15. The chief voice tells them that they never **<u>reckoned</u>** on the magician going invisible too:
    a. to move in a stealthy manner; slink
    b. to listen secretly to a private conversation
    c. to fall back into a former state
    d. to count, compute, or calculate

II. Matching: Place the letter of the correct answer in the blank:

1._____ extracted   A. the state or quality of being foolish

2._____ mallets   B. offering or suggesting something for acceptance

3._____ dreadful   C. and abrupt, exclamatory utterance

4._____ folly   D. causing great dread, fear, or terror

5._____ parley   E. absolute; frankly direct; straightforward

6._____ enmity   F. to get, pull, or draw out, usually with special effort

7._____ ejaculations   G. an informal conference with an enemy under a truce

8._____ baccy   H. a hammer like tool with a head commonly of wood

9._____ proposal   I. a feeling or condition of hostility; hatred; ill will

10._____ downright   J. and in formal name for tobacco

III. Matching: Place the letter of the correct answer in the blank:

1._____ deceive   A. an alcoholic liquor derived from honey and water

2._____ muck   B. To listen secretly to a private conversation

3._____ flagged   C. Food supplies; provisions

4._____ victuals   D. Mix things together in a confused and disordered way

5._____ mead   E. To mislead by a false appearance or statement

6._____ fury   F. Any hard stone that splits and is suitable for paving

7._____ muddlesome   G. Filth, dirt, or slime

8._____ eavesdropping   H. Unrestrained or violent anger, rage, passion or the like

<u>**VOYAGE OF THE DAWN TREADER**</u>
<u>**VOCABULARY TEST CHAPTERS 7-10**</u>
<u>**ANSWER KEY**</u>

I.   **Multiple Choice:**
1. b
2. d
3. c
4. b
5. c
6. b
7. d
8. a
9. c
10. b
11. d
12. a
13. c
14. b
15. d

II. **Matching:**
1. F
2. H
3. D
4. A
5. G
6. I
7. C
8. J
9. B
10. E

III. **Matching:**
1. E
2. G
3. F
4. C
5. A
6. H
7. D
8. B

VOYAGE OF THE DAWN TREADER
VOCABULARY TEST CHAPTERS 11-12

I.   Fill in the Blank: Use the Word Bank below to fill in the blanks:

1. Eustace said he wished the magician had made the Duffers _____ instead of invisible.

2. Reepicheep told them if they turned back for fear of the darkness it would be an _____ of all their honors.

3. In front of the lantern Lucy could see the black shape of Drinian crouching at the _____.

4. Reepicheep asks Caspian how he can tolerate this _____.

5. When all the men run for the oars Reepicheep says it is a panic, it is a _____.

6. When Lucy cries out to Aslan to send them how, help shows up in the form of an _____.

7. The magician explains to Lucy that he made the Duffers into _____.

8. Lucy's conscience _____ her when she saw their anxious faces and realized how long she had forgotten them.

9. The magician laid out to blank sheets of _____ on the table, and as Drinian spoke he drew lines that became a map of all the places they had been.

10. When Lucy and the magician realized Aslan was gone they were both quite _____.

Word Bank:

monopods	impeachment	crestfallen	mutiny	smote
rout	tiller	parchment	albatross	inaudible

II. Matching: Place the letter of the correct answer in the blank:

1._____girdle   A. Lighted or shining with an unnatural, fiery glow

2._____trudging   B. Marked by utter cowardice

3._____sleepers   C. A belts, cord, sash, warned about the waist

4._____boatswain   D. extreme or terminal point, limit or part of something

5._____lurid   E. To walk, especially wearily; tramp

6._____extrmity   F. a petty officer on a merchant vessel, in charge of Rigging

7._____poltroonery   G. Timber or beam serving as foundation for the rails

VOYAGE OF THE DAWN TREADER
VOCABULARY TEST CHAPTERS 11-12
ANSWER KEY

I. **Fill in the Blank:**
1. Inaudible
2. Impeachment
3. Tiller
4. Mutiny
5. Rout
6. Albatross
7. Monopods
8. Smote
9. Parchment
10. Crestfallen

II. **Matching:**
1. C
2. E
3. G
4. F
5. A
6. D
7. B

VOYAGE OF THE DAWN TREADER
VOCABULARY TEST CHAPTERS 13-16

I. **Multiple Choice: Circle the letter of the correct answer:**

1. When they tried to decide where to sit, they **sauntered** around and around the table:
    a. to act or proceed with unwarrantable or in pertinent boldness
    b. to dispose of personal property by last will
    c. to walk with a leisurely gait; stroll
    d. firm in purpose or intent; determined

2. Ramandu asks Caspian if he is **resolved** to sell further east and return to break the enchantment:
    a. involving or full of grave risk or peril; hazardous, dangerous
    b. firm in purpose or intent; determined
    c. causing great pain or suffering
    d. weakened by old age; feeble; infirm

3. The level Valley which lay at the head of the bay showed no road or track or other sign of **habitation**:
    a. a landing place constructed along the edge of a body of water; wharf
    b. an uninterrupted on interrupted space or area; a wide extent of anything
    c. a period of time spent doing something
    d. a place of residence; abode

4. There were **flagons** of gold and silver and curiously wrought glass:
    a. a large bottle for wine, liquors, etc.
    b. a ray or beam
    c. the handle of a sword or dagger
    d. a small crown

5. When they saw a Ramandu, he looked so mild and **grave** that all the travelers rose to their feet and stood in silence:
    a. weakened by old age; feeble; infirm
    b. firm in purpose or intent; determined
    c. serious or solemn; sober
    d. doubtful; infirm of purpose; vacillating

6. Most of them talked far into the night or hung over the ship's side watching the **luminous** dance of the foam thrown up by their bows:
    a. living under the surface of the sea
    b. a layer of matted Earth formed by grass and plant roots
    c. a legendary sea monster causing large whirlpool off the coast of Norway
    d. radiating or reflecting light; shining; bright

7. They took some time choosing their seats at the **perilous** table:
    a. firm in purpose or intent; determined
    b. involving or full of grave risk or peril; hazardous; dangerous
    c. serious or solemn; sober
    d. causing great pain or suffering

8. Caspian said that every man that comes with them shall **bequeath** the title of the *Dawn Treader* to all his descendants:
   a. to dispose of personal property by last will
   b. to rebuke severely
   c. to act or proceed with unwarrantable or in pertinent boldness
   d. to put ashore and abandoned on a desolate island by way of punishment

9. Lucy realized what she was seeing was a **submarine** forest:
   a. a place of residence; dwelling; abode
   b. a landing place constructed along the edge of a body of water; wharf
   c. living under the surface of the sea
   d. a ray or beam

10. The reckless hunters and brave Knights of the sea go down into the depths on **quests** and adventures:
    a. a small crown
    b. a period of time spent doing something
    c. an uninterrupted space or area; a wide extent of anything
    d. an adventurous expedition undertaken by knight secure or achieve something

11. The figure carried a light and this light was really all they could see **distinctly**:
    a. firm in purpose or intent; determine
    b. without doubt; unmistakable
    c. weakened by old age; feeble; infirm
    d. doubtful; infirm of purpose; vacillating

12. Ramandu tells them that in this island there is sleep without **stint** or measure:
    a. an uninterrupted space or area; a wide extent of anything
    b. sudden or complete loss of courage; other disheartened meant
    c. a period of time spent doing something
    d. a layer of matted earth formed by grass and plant roots

13. Drinian said Reepicheep should be keel hauled and **marooned** and have his whiskers cut off :
    a. to rebuke severely
    b. to dispose of personal property by last will
    c. to put ashore and abandon on a desolate island by way of punishment
    d. to act or proceed with unwarrantable or in pertinent boldness

14. Drinian asked Caspian if he was **abdicating:**
    a. to renounce or relinquish a throne, especially in a formal manner
    b. to dispose of personal property by last will
    c. to walk with a leisurely gait; stroll
    d. to rebuke severely

15. Then all in one moment there was a **rending** of the blue wall and a terrible white light from beyond the sky:
    a. to act or proceed with unwarrantable or impertinent boldness
    b. to rebuke severely
    c. to dispose of personal property by last will
    d. to tear apart, split, or divide

II.   Matching: Place the letter of the correct answer in the blank:

1. ____ Botany   A. An uninterrupted space or area

2. ____ Turf   B. The handle of a sword or dagger

3. ____ hilt   C. A lofty, often slender, tower or turret attached to a
                                 Mosque

4. ____ Decrepit   D. A layer of matted earth formed by grass and plant roots

5. ____ Oblivion   E. A ray or beam

6. ____ Quay   F. The science of plants

7. ____ expanse   G. A relatively small, upright structure, commonly
                                 terminating in a gable, a pyramid, or a cone

8. ____ shafts   H. the state of forgetting or of being oblivious

9. ____ pinnacles   I. weakened by old age; feeble; infirm

10. ____ minarets   J. a landing place constructed along the edge of a body of
                                 water; wharf

III.   Matching: Place the letter of the correct answer in the blank:

1. ____ Kraken   A. A meeting for deliberation, discussion, or decision

2. ____ keel hauled   B. to act or proceed with unwarrantable or impertinent
                                 boldness

3. ____ Coronet   C. a legendary sea monster causing large whirlpools off
                                 the coast of Norway

4. ____ consultation   D. causing great pain or suffering

5. ____ dismay   E. to rebuke severely

6. ____ presume   F. doubtful; infirm of purpose; vacillating

7. ____ irresolute   G. a small crown

8. ____ grievous   H. sudden or complete loss of courage; utter
                                 disheartenment

VOYAGE OF THE DAWN TREADER
VOCABULARY TEST CHAPTERS 13-16
ANSWER KEY

I.   **Multiple Choice:**
1. c
2. b
3. d
4. a
5. c
6. d
7. b
8. a
9. c
10. d
11. b
12. c
13. c
14. a
15. d

II. **Matching:**
1. F
2. D
3. B
4. I
5. H
6. J
7. A
8. E
9. G
10. C

III. **Matching:**
1. C
2. E
3. G
4. A
5. H
6. B
7. F
8. D

VOYAGE OF THE DAWN TREADER
TEST

I.   Multiple Choice: Circle the letter of the correct answer:

1. Which of the following is **not** one of the main characters in this story:
    a.   Edmund Pevensie
    b.   Susan Pevensie
    c.   Eustace Clarence Scrubb
    d.   Lucy Pevensie

2. How did the children get into Narnia?
    a.   Through the back of a wardrobe
    b.   Being jerked off a railway station
    c.   Going through a stone gate
    d.   Jumping into a ship in a picture

3. When they first come aboard the *Dawn Treader*, Eustace has the most trouble with:
    a.   Caspian
    b.   Drinian
    c.   Reepicheep
    d.   Edmund

4. What is the purpose of the voyage of the *Dawn Treader*?
    a.   Look for buried pirate treasure
    b.   Find seven lords exiled by Caspian's uncle & rescue them
    c.   Chart unknown territories
    d.   Discover and claim new lands

5. What does Eustace decide to do about his frustration?
    a.   Keep a diary
    b.   Sue Caspian
    c.   Take up boxing
    d.   Phone his parents

6. Why do the Lone Islands belong to Narnia?
    a.   They were conquered by High King Peter
    b.   They have always belonged to Narnia
    c.   They came under Narnia's control during the White Witch's reign
    d.   No one really knows

7. Who are the first men they meet on the Lone Islands?
    a.   A group of fishermen
    b.   Lord Bern and his followers
    c.   Governor Gumpas and his guards
    d.   A group of slavers

8. How does Lord Bern recognize Caspian?
    a.   The color of his hair and his eyes
    b.   The look of his face and sound of his voice
    c.   The shape of his nose and cleft in his chin
    d.   All of the above

9. Why is it important for Lord Bern to recognize Caspian?
   a. He is one of the men for whom Caspian is searching
   b. Caspian is his king
   c. It is necessary for Caspian to gain his loyalty to win the Islands
   d. All of the above

10. Before he enters the Governor's palace, Caspian:
    a. Ties up the Palace Guard
    b. Attacks the Palace Guard
    c. Gains the loyalty of the Palace Guard
    d. Sends the Palace Guard away

11. When Gumpas refuses to end the slave trade, what is the consequence of his action?
    a. He loses his job
    b. He is put in jail
    c. He is exiled
    d. He is sent back to Narnia for trial

12. When Lord Bern asks Caspian to remain on the Lone Islands and help them in case of war with the Calormens, his reply is:
    a. I have an oath to fulfill
    b. what would I tell Reepicheep?
    c. Neither a nor b
    d. both a and b

13. When Eustace tries to sneak an extra drink of water in the middle of the night what happens?
    a. He is caught by Edmund
    b. he is caught by Reepicheep
    c. he is caught by Lucy
    d. he is caught by Drinian

14. What happens to Eustace when he tries to get away alone to nap while the others are working on the ship?
    a. He is turned into a sea monster
    b. he is turned into a mouse
    c. he is turned into a dog
    d. he is turned into a dragon

15. When Eustace realizes he has the power to get even with Edmund and Caspian, what does he recognize?
    a. He wants to consume them with his fire
    b. he would rather be their friend then get even with them
    c. he can set a trap for them in the dragon's lair
    d. none of the above

16. What does Lucy do to try to help Eustace?
    a. She tries to cast a spell on him
    b. she wraps his arms in the bandage
    c. she tries to get the bracelet off
    d. she treats his arm with her cordial

17. How does being in the dragon's skin change the way the others feel about Eustace?
    a. He is not so annoying
    b. he is trying to help them
    c. they feel sorry for him because he's trapped in the Dragon skin
    d. all of the above

18. Who becomes the closest to Eustace during the time he is a dragon?
    a. Reepicheep
    b. Lucy
    c. Edmund
    d. Caspian

19. When Eustace becomes a boy again who is the first person he tells?
    a. Reepicheep
    b. Lucy
    c. Edmund
    d. Caspian

20. Who does Eustace meet that changes him from a dragon back into a boy?
    a. Trumpkin
    b. Aslan
    c. Octesian
    d. Tumnus

21. What instruction is Eustace given that he finds perplexing?
    a. To remove his scales
    b. to remove his skin
    c. to remove his clothing
    d. to remove his horns

22. because of the golden man they find at the bottom of the pool on the next island they named this island:
    a. Goldwater Island
    b. Deathwater Island
    c. Treasure Island
    d. Escape Island

23. When they land on the island with the Duffers, what is the first sign that the island is inhabited?
    a. Smoke rising from the chimney of the house
    b. The kept appearance of the lawns
    c. the spear
    d. the voices heard by Lucy

24. Why do the Duffers need Lucy?
    a. They need a girl her age to lift the spell of divisibility that is on them
    b. they need a girl of her age to lift the spell of inaudibility that is on them
    c. they need a girl of her age to lift the spell of invincibility that is on
    d. they need a girl of her age to lift the spell of invisibility that is on them

25. When Lucy wants to use the spell that would make her more beautiful than any mortal she is stopped by whom?
    a. Aslan
    b. the magician
    c. Caspian
    d. Edmund

26. Lucy is hurt because she does what that is wrong?
    a. Lies
    b. steals
    c. eavesdrops
    d. gossips

27. How does the magician feel about those over whom he has to rule?
    a. He looks forward to the day he will not have to use magic to rule over them
    b. he thinks they're stupid but harmless
    c. he looks forward to the day he can rule over them with wisdom
    d. all of the above

28. What causes both the magician and Lucy to feel sad?
    a. Caspian abandons them
    b. Aslan leaves
    c. the Duffers run away
    d. Edmund leaves

29. Why did the magician cast the spell on the Duffers?
    a. He was angry with them
    b. they were too stupid
    c. they were disobedient
    d. he just felt like it

30. What two things does the magician do to help out on their journey?
    a. Draws a map and repairs their bow
    b. draws a map and makes them invisible
    c. draws a map and re-fuels the *Dawn Treader*
    d. draws a map and repairs their stern

31. When Caspian considers turning back from the area of great darkness, he decides to go ahead when Reepicheep says what?
    a. He would not want to report in Narnia that they were afraid of the dark
    b. he is braver than all of the men on board the ship
    c. the people in Narnia will make fun of all of them if they turned back
    d. none of the above

32. When Lucy cries out to Aslan for help what does he send?
    a. Himself
    b. an albatross
    c. a dove
    d. a seagull

33. Which Lord do they find in the darkness?
    a. Lord Argoz
    b. Lord Revilian
    c. Lord Mavramorn
    d. Lord Rhoop

34. When he tells the men he has been on an island where dreams come to life, what is the reaction?
    a. They rush to the oars and begin to row
    b. Reepicheep declares the men's actions a mutiny
    c. Caspian orders the men to row faster
    d. all of the above

35. When they land on Ramandu's island, how does Lucy describe the smell?
    a. Spring flowers
    b. a purple kind of smell
    c. smell of roses
    d. gardenias

36. When they first find the three sleeping lords around the table what do they believe is the source of the enchantment?
    a. The water
    b. the air
    c. food
    d. the flowers

37. why do they decide to spend the night sitting around the table?
    a. Caspian challenges them
    b. Reepicheep challenges them
    c. Edmund challenges them
    d. Eustace challenges them

38. What does Lucy recall about the Knife of Stone?
    a. She saw at one time in her world
    b. she heard about it in the story
    c. she read about it in a fairytale
    d. she saw the White Witch use it to kill Aslan

39. What solution does Ramandu offer for Lord Rhoop while Caspian is sailing further east?
    a. Ramandu will give him healing rest on the island while Caspian is gone
    b. he can work there until Caspian returns
    c. he can marry Raman dues daughter
    d. none of the above

40. What does Lucy see under the water that no one else notices?
    a. Sea serpent
    b. sharks
    c. Sea People
    d. Dolphins

41. When Reepicheep jumps into the water what is he excited about?
    a. He notices the Sea People
    b. he discovers the water is sweet
    c. he swallows too much water
    d. he discovers is an oil spill in the water

42. What is important about the water?
    a. It makes them feel strong
    b. it allows them to look into the sun
    c. it allows them to go without eating
    d. all of the above

43. What does Caspian find interesting about Edmund and Lucy's world?
    a. It's part of the solar system
    b. its round
    c. it revolves around the sun
    d. none of the above

44. What does Aslan tell Lucy and Edmund about their ability to return to Narnia?
    a. They will return to Narnia one more time
    b. they will return to Narnia two more times
    c. they will not return to Narnia again
    d. they will return to Narnia as many times as they want

45. The character who has changed the most by the end of the book is:
    a. Lucy
    b. Edmund
    c. Eustace
    d. Caspian

II.   **Matching: Place the letter of the correct answer in the blank:**

1.____Eustace   A. Captain of the *Dawn Treader*

2.____Lucy   B. noble exiled by Miraz found on the Lone Islands

3.____Edmund   C. talking mouse – brave knight of Narnia

4.____Caspian   D. owner of the bracelet worn by dragon

5.____Reepicheep   E. former High King of Narnia

6.____Drinian   F. former star who is currently in a state of resting

7.____Lord Rhoop   G. difficult boy who was turned into a dragon

8.____Lord Bern   H. current King of Narnia

9.____Lord Octesian   I. former High Queen of Narnia

10.____Ramandu   J. exiled noble who lived on the island of dreams

III. Discution: Choose five of the following questions and discuss them thoroughly:

1. Discuss the character of Eustace Scrubbs: What kind of a character is it, how is it developed? How does his character change in the course of the story?

2. Why is the scene in which Eustace is changed from a dragon back into a boy important? How is it accomplished? What does this illustrate?

3. What was the lesson of the Duffers? Why was it important?

4. What did Lucy learn when she eavesdropped on her two friends? What did Aslan tell her? What is the lesson?

5. When Eustace had the opportunity to get revenge on Caspian and Edmund, what did he discover? Explain what this says about human nature.

6. Describe the climax of the book and why the main conflict of the book occurs at the same time.

7. What does Aslan tell Lucy and Edmund that makes them sad? How does he alleviate this pain?

VOYAGE OF THE DAWN TREADER
TEST ANSWER KEY

I.   **Multiple Choice:**

1. B
2. D
3. C
4. B
5. A
6. C
7. D
8. B
9. D
10. C
11. A
12. D
13. B
14. D
15. B
16. D
17. D
18. A
19. C
20. B
21. C
22. B
23. B
24. D
25. A
26. C
27. D
28. B
29. C
30. D
31. A
32. B
33. D
34. D
35. B
36. C
37. B
38. D
39. A
40. C
41. B
42. D
43. B
44. C
45. C

II. Matching:
1. G
2. I
3. E
4. H
5. C
6. A
7. J
8. B
9. D
10. F

III. Discussion:

1. Eustace Clarence Scrubbs is a dynamic character. He changes dramatically from the beginning of the book to the end. In the beginning of the book he is described as a child who spent more time reading books than playing outside with other children. He had no friends. He was whiney and complaining. After he is turned into a dragon, he realizes how difficult he has been and how much he longs for the friendship of others. His character undergoes a transformation to the point that, even when he returns to his state as a child, he tries to fight against a sea serpent and wants to do his part instead of shirking his duty.

2. The scene in which Eustace is changed back into a boy is important because it is an illustration of salvation. Aslan comes to Eustace and tells him to come to a well and remove his clothing. Eustace understands that, as a dragon, he must remove his skin. He tries three times to do it on his own, but is unable. He finally has to allow Aslan to do it for him, just as we must submit to Christ to remove our sins from us and provide us with a new life through Him. Eustace is made into a new boy, just as we are new creatures in Christ. Aslan clothes him in new clothing, just as we are clothed in the righteousness of God when we are saved.

3. The Duffers were turned invisible as a result of their disobedience to the magician. This is an illustration of the fact that we are to be obedient to God and to those who are in authority above us. If we are disobedient, we have to suffer the consequences.

4. When Lucy eavesdropped on her two friends she was hurt because of thing she heard. Aslan told her that even eavesdropping through magic is still wrong. The lesson is that things we hear when we are listening to people and they don't know we're hearing them can lead to misunderstandings, which can cause hurt feelings and broken relationships.

5. Eustace discovered that he would rather have the friendship of Caspian and Edmund than to get even with them. This shows that human beings were created as social beings. God intended for us to have relationships with other people. The desire of our heart is to enjoy the close relationships with others. Eustace was finding this out. It is not fun to be on the outside all the time, and to take revenge on Edmund and Caspian would have simply kept him on the outside longer.

6. The climax of the book occurs when Caspian must decide whether to continue on with Reepicheep to Aslan's land at the end of the world or return to Narnia and fulfill his responsibilities as King. This is also the main conflict of the book. Although there have been conflicts of man against nature and man against man the main conflict occurs within Caspian as man against himself. Caspian must ultimately decide to fulfill the responsibility of his own destiny.

7. Aslan tells Lucy and Edmund they will not return to Narnia because they are too old. This makes them very sad. He tells them they will know him in their land by another name. He tells them they were brought to Narnia so that they would know him there for a little while in order to know him and their world by the name he goes by there.

Voyage of the Dawn Treader
Vocab Chapter 1-2

www.CrosswordWeaver.com

ACROSS

1 to incine to one side; careen
3 A square rigged, round bottomed boat used mainly for bulk trade
4 unusual or strante; odd; different
6 a person who abstains totally from intoxicating drink
7 To spread out, expand, or extend
9 take revenge on behalf of
12 To bring a charge or accusation against someone
13 Large, fast sailing ships of the middle ages
15 the forepart of a ship or boat
18 An officer on a warship, or a petty officer on a merchant vessel, in charge of rigging, anchors, etc.
19 A person who is opposed to war or violence of any kind
20 Of the human body; bodily; physical

23 a strenuous effort; attempt
25 A small sword, having a narrow blade and used for thrusting
27 A distance of about 3 miles
30 The quality of being new and fresh and interesting
32 One who seizes power without proper authority
33 Moody, surly, morose, churlish
34 marked by lack of taste, culture, etc.
35 The final settlement of a matter

DOWN

2 A large sailing vessel of the 15th to the 17th century's used as a fighting or merchant ship
3 the act or ceremony of crowning a monarch
5 covered or highlighted with gold
6 A very short time; an instant

8 terrifying; horrible
10 extraordinarily fine or admirable
11 The part of a vessel at the bow where the crew is quartered
14 A superstructure at the stern of a vessel
16 showing bad manners; impolite; rude
17 the use of the same vowel sound with different consonants
21 salty
22 the kitchen of a ship, boat, or aircraft
24 Bending readily without breaking or becoming deformed
26 A merchant vessel having various rigs
28 A wretched coward; Craven
29 of less than normal size and strengy; weak
31 food supplies; provisions

WORD BANK: Assonance, avenge, boatswain, briny, carracks, cogs, coronation, corporal, discourteous, disposition, dromonds, endeavours, exquisite, forecastle, galleons, galley, ghastly, gilded, leagues, listing, lodge, novelty, pacifist, poltroon, poop, prow, puny, rapier, singularly, splayed, sulkily, supple, teetotalers, trice, usurper, victual, vulgar.

Voyage of the Dawn Treader

Vocab Chapter 1-2

Solution:

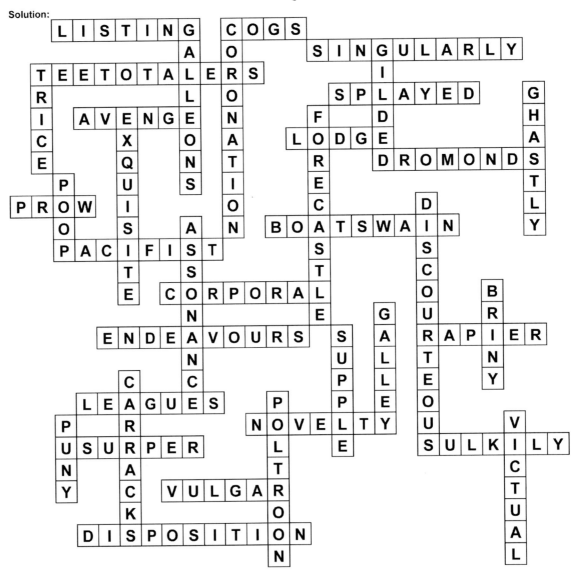

Voyage of the Dawn Treader

Vocabulary 3-4

www.CrosswordWeaver.com

ACROSS

2 To twist the body about, or squirm, as in pain
6 Rottenness; anything vile
8 To permit, approve, or agree
10 A carefree, worthless, or irresponsible person; rogue
13 A set of incoherent or pointless statements; garbled nonsense
17 A layer of matted Earth formed by grass and plant roots
21 Affecting extreme elegance in dress and manner
22 To make furious; enrage
23 To be or become weak or feeble; droop; fade
24 Wearing a medieval protective glove
25 Out of the way; secluded

DOWN

1 A back door or gate
3 Irritating, exasperating, or bitterly humiliating
4 The lower classes; the common people
5 A landing pier; dock
7 Limp and soiled, as with rain or dirt
8 One vessel or ship accompanying another
9 A collection or file of documents containing detailed information about a person or topic
11 To smother
12 A search or pursuit made in order to find or obtain something
14 Repugnantly hateful; detestable; loathsome
15 A period of 14 consecutive days; two weeks
16 pay out, especially for expenses; expend
18 Not lived in or on
19 A beating administered with a whip or rod
20 A territory held in fee

WORD BANK: Abominable, bedraggled, carrion, consented, consorts, dandified, dispersedto, dossiers, fief, flogging, fortnight, galling, gauntleted, infuriated, jetty, languishing, postern, quest, rabble, remote, rigmarole, suffocated, turf, uninhabited, vagabonds, writhing.

Voyage of the Dawn Treader

Vocabulary 3-4

Solution:

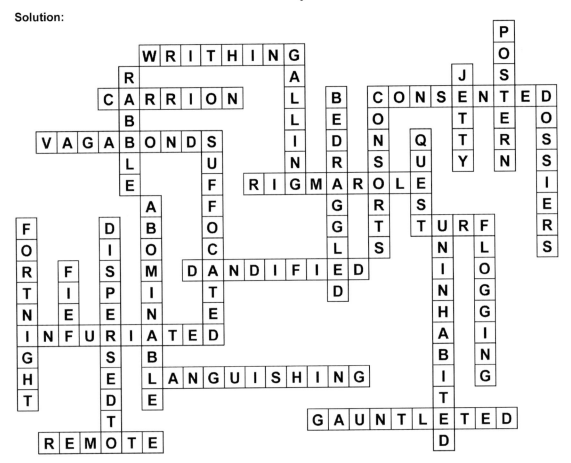

Voyage of the Dawn Treader

Vocabulary 5-6

www.CrosswordWeaver.com

ACROSS

3 A close-fitting jacket or short coat, usually sleeveless
4 The four-part of a ship or boat; bow
7 A descent of water over a steep surface
8 To shorten a sail by tying in one or more reefs
10 person who is smugly and self righteously narrowminded
11 causing anxiety or uneasiness; disturbiing
15 a supply or accumulation that is hidden or guarded
20 A contemptible worthless person
22 bending readily; pliant; limber; supple; flexible
23 To board a ship, aircraft, or other vehicle as for a journey
24 To turn, swing, twist

DOWN

1 Causing dismay or horror
2 To cause a vessel to incline to one side
5 Radio
6 a long, narrow arm of the sea bordered by steep cliffs
9 A diabolically cruel or wicked person
10 A cliff with a vertical, nearly vertical, or overhanging face
12 characterized by great caution, secrecy, etc
13 Having a superior manner; condescending
14 Highly offensive; repugnant; disgusting
16 A thick soled, laced boot or half boot
17 Burden some, unjustly harsh, or tyrannical
18 to make a false show of something; pretend
19 Bad, evil, base, or wicked
20 To cover a hatch so as to make watertight
21 Lonely and sad; forsaken

WORD BANK: Appalling, battened, blighter, buskins, cataract, disquieting, embarked, fiends, fjord, forlorn, hoard, jerkins, listing, lithbending, odious, oppressive, patronizing, precipices, priga, prow, reef, shamming, sinister, slewed, stealthily, wireless.

111

Voyage of the Dawn Treader

Vocabulary 5-6

Solution:

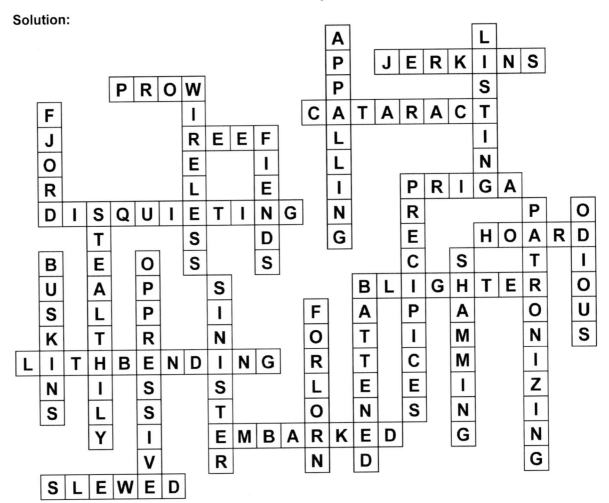

Voyage of the Dawn Treader
Vocabulary 7-10

www.CrosswordWeaver.com

ACROSS

2 To get, pull, or draw out, usually with special effort
4 Easily seen or noticed; readily visible
5 Any hard stone that splits and is suitable for paving
9 Absolute; frankly direct; straightforward
11 A hammer like tool with ahead commonly of wood
12 Boldness or determination when facing danger
13 Of or pertaining to human beings as subject to death; human
14 And alcoholic liquor made by fermenting honey and water
16 A gallery our passage connecting parts of a building; hallway
19 Unqualified or absolute

22 To move in a stealthy manner; slink
23 Unrestrained or violent anger, rage, passion, or the like
25 An abrupt, exclamatory utterance
26 The state or quality of being foolish
28 Food supplies; provisions
29 Given to inquiry, research, or asking questions
31 To mislead by a false appearance or statement; delude
32 An informal name for tobacco

DOWN

1 Filth, dirt, or slime
3 An act of falling back into a former state or practice
4 A small roundish boat made of skins stretched on a wicker frame

6 Causing great dread, fear, or terror
7 A facial expression, often ugly or contorted
8 A brilliant red
10 Characterized by faithlessness or readiness to betray trust; traitorous
15 To listen secretly to a private conversation
17 To count, compute, or calculate
18 Two makes things together in a confused or disordered way
20 Absolutely trustworthy or sure
21 The act of offering are suggesting something for acceptance
24 To hold an informal conference with an enemy under a truce
27 a feeling or condition of hostility; hatred; ill will
30 Eager; interested; enthusiastic

WORD BANK: Baccy, conspicuous, coracle, corridor, deceive, downright, dreadful, eavesdropping, ejaculations, enmity, extracted, flagged, folly, fury, grimace, infallible, inquisitive, keen, mallets, mead, mortals, muck, muddlesome, parley, proposal, reckoned, relapses, skulking, treacherous, unmitigated, valor, vermilions, victuals.

Voyage of the Dawn Treader

Vocabulary 7-10

Solution:

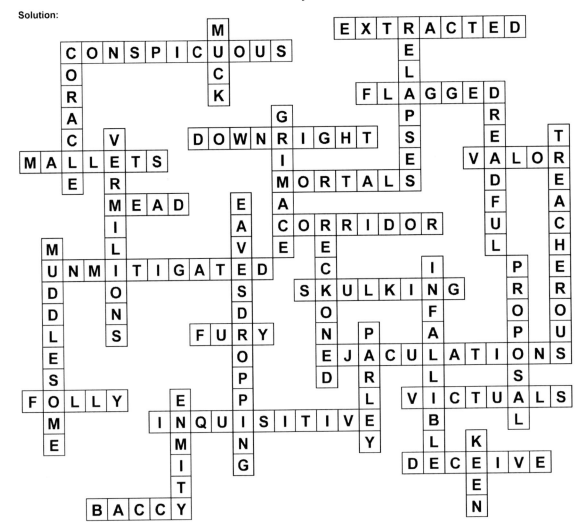

Voyage of the Dawn Treader

Vocabulary 11-12

www.CrosswordWeaver.com

ACROSS

1 Marked by utter cowardice
4 The extreme or terminal point, limit, or part of something
7 A belts, cord, sash or the like, warn about the waste
12 To affect mentally or morally with a sudden pang
13 A large web footed seabird that has the ability to remain aloft for long periods
15 Demonstration that a witness is less worthy of belief
16 Lighted or shining with an unnatural, fiery glow
17 To walk especially wearily; tramp

DOWN

2 A bar or lever used for turning the rudder in steering
3 Rebellion against any authority, especially sailors against officers
5 A species with only one leg
6 Timber or beam serving as a foundation or support for the rails
8 Dejected; dispirited; discouraged
9 The officer on a ship in charge of rigging, anchors, etc.
10 Incapable of being heard
11 This skin of sheep, goats, etc. prepared for use as material on which to write
14 A defeat attended with disorderly flight

WORD BANK: Albatross, boatswain, crestfallen, extremity, girdle, impeachment, inaudible, lurid, monopod, mutiny, parchment, poltroonery, rout, sleepers, smote, tiller, trudging.

Voyage of the Dawn Treader

Vocabulary 11-12

Solution:

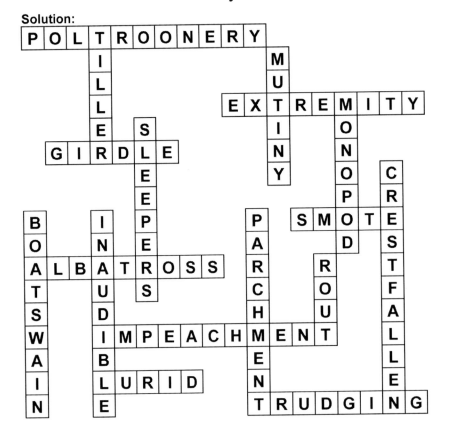

Voyage of the Dawn Treader
Vocabulary 13-16

www.CrosswordWeaver.com

ACROSS

1 A lofty, often slender tower or turret attached to a mosque
4 The handle of a sword or dagger
8 A layer of message Earth formed by grass and plant roots
11 Serious or solemn; sober
12 An uninterrupted space or area; a wide extent of anything
13 A relatively small, upright structure terminating in a gable, a pyramid, or a cone
15 Sudden or complete loss of courage; utter disheartenment
17 Firm in purpose or intent; determined
18 weakened by old age; feeble; infirm
19 A legendary sea monster causing large whirlpools off the coast of Norway

23 To tear apart, split, or divide
24 To put ashore and abandon on a desolate island by way of punishment
27 A ray or beam
28 A small crown
30 Causing great pain or suffering
31 A meeting for deliberation, discussion, or decision
32 The science of plants
33 A period of time spent doing something

DOWN

2 Living under the surface of the sea
3 Without doubt; unmistakably
5 An adventurous expedition undertaken by a knight to secure or achieve something
6 To rebuke severely

7 Radiating or reflecting light; shining; bright
9 A place of residence; dwelling; abode
10 To dispose of personal property by last will
14 To walk with a leisurely gait; stroll
16 Doubtful; infirm of purpose; vacillating
20 To renounce or relinquish a throne, especially in a formal manner
21 A large bottle for wine, liquors, etc.
22 To act or proceed with unwarrantable or impertinent boldness
25 The state of forgetting or of being oblivious
26 Involving or full of grave risk or peril; hazardous
29 A landing place constructed along the edge of a body of water; wharf

WORD BANK: Abdicating, bequeath, botany, consultation, coronet, decrepit, dismay, distinctively, expanse, flagons, grave, grievous, habitation, hilt, irresolute, keelhauled, kraken, luminous, marooned, minarets, oblivion, perilous, pinnacles, presume, quay, quests, rending, resolved, sauntered, shafts, stint, submarine, turf.

Voyage of the Dawn Treader

Vocabulary 13-16

Solution:

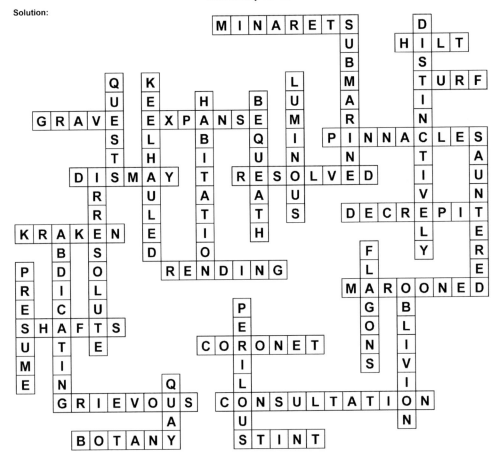

SELECTED BIBLIOGRAPHY

Biographical Material

http://www.cslewis.org/resources/chronoccl.html. (2006)

Lindsley, Art. http://www.cslewisinstitute.org/pages/resources/cslewis/index.php. (2006)

Sayer, George. Jack: C.S. Lewis and His Times. San Francisco: Harper and Row, Publishers. 1988.

Dictionaries:

Slater, Rosalie J. Noah Webster's 1828 American Dictionary of the English Language. (San Francisco: Foundation for American Christian Education); 1967 & 1995.

Webster's Third International Dictionary (Springfield, MA: G & C. Merriam CO.); 1963.

Webster's Universal College Dictionary (New York: Gramercy Books); 1997.

http://www.dictionary.com/html (2013).